Common Trees
of the
Highveld

R. B. Drummond
and
Keith Coates Palgrave

Water colour paintings by the late
Olive H. Coates Palgrave

Photographs by
Deric and Paul Coates Palgrave

D1732756

Longman Rhodesia

Longman Rhodesia (Pvt) Ltd
Beatrice Road, Southerton, Salisbury

*Associated companies, branches and
representatives throughout the world*

First published 1973

ISBN 0 582 64106 3

Printed in Rhodesia by Mardon Printers (Pvt) Limited, Salisbury

Contents

Introduction

In this book there are described and illustrated fifty-four trees which are commonly encountered in the woodlands of the Rhodesian highveld.

The term *highveld* is difficult to define exactly and, for the purpose of this book, we have taken it to include the land lying to either side of the central watershed, stretching from Umtali in the east to the Matopos in the west, and generally at an altitude above 1 100 m, but not including the mountain areas in the eastern parts of the country. Within this somewhat loose framework there are certain areas which, as far as vegetation is concerned, present anomalies: Umtali itself is verging on the lowveld, while also providing links with the mountainous areas of the Eastern Districts, and the flora of the Gatooma area is strongly influenced by the Zambezi valley vegetation which has intruded up the valleys of the Umniati and Umfuli rivers. By confining the scope of this book within these limits, we hope that the way has been left open for future publications, perhaps *Common Trees of the Rhodesian Lowveld*, and possibly *Common Trees of the Eastern Mountains*.

In Rhodesia there are over seven hundred species of trees which are indigenous to the country, and of these a fairly large proportion may be found in the area which we have defined as the highveld. Therefore it is clear that the species covered in this book are far from comprehensive. A number of factors have limited the choice of the trees to be included, not least of which is the size of the book itself. The following is a list of the trees which are relatively common, but which, regrettably, have had to be excluded:

ANACARDIACEAE
Rhus lancea, R. leptodictya, R. longipes, and *R. quartiniana*
APOCYNACEAE
Rauvolfia caffra
CELASTRACEAE
Cassine matabelica, and *C. transvaalensis*

COMPOSITAE
Vernonia ampla, V. amygdalina, and *V. bellinghamii*
EBENACEAE
Euclea crispa, E. divinorum, and *E. natalensis*
Diospyros natalensis subsp. *nummularia,* and *D. lycioides* subsp. *sericea*
Schrebera alata
FLACOURTIACEAE
Scolopia zeyheri
Flacourtia indica
Dovyalis zeyheri
GUTTIFERAE
Garcinia huillensis
HETEROPYXIDACEAE
Heteropyxis dehniae
LEGUMINOSAE
Elephantorrhiza goetzei
Dalbergia melanoxylon, and *D. nitidula*
Ormocarpum kirkii
MYRICACEAE
Myrica serrata
OLEACEAE
Olea africana
PITTOSPORACEAE
Pittosporum viridiflorum
RUBIACEAE
Hymenodictyon floribundum
Rothmannia fischeri
SAPINDACEAE
Zanha africana
SAPOTACEAE
Bequaertiodendron magalismontanum
TILIACEAE
Grewia monticola
ULMACEAE
Celtis africana
UMBELLIFERAE
Heteromorpha arborescens
VERBENACEAE
Clerodendrum glabrum

in a number of cases, while the tree might be commonly encountered in certain areas of the highveld, it is more typically a tree of the lowveld and so it has been excluded from the present volume. Trees which would fall into this category are:

LEGUMINOSAE
Afzelia quanzensis
Burkea africana
Lonchocarpus capassa
MELIACEAE
Khaya nyasica
PALMAE
Phoenix reclinata
SAPINDACEAE
Pappea capensis
SAPOTACEAE
Mimusops zeyheri

The trees which are described in this book are all indigenous to Rhodesia and no exotic trees have been included. There are many trees, however, which have been introduced into the country at some time in the past. These can be divided into two categories: those which have been planted but which show no tendency to become naturalised, and those which regenerate readily and are able to compete with the natural vegetation. Fortunately, most of the cultivated trees fall into the first category and include all the species of *Eucalyptus* and all the coniferous trees such as the pines and cypresses. In the second category is *Duranta repens*, the forget-me-not tree, which is an example of a garden shrub or small tree, the fruits of which have been spread by birds so successfully that it is now a common tree on termite mounds in the Rhodesian highveld. Trees such as *Toona ciliata* and *Jacaranda mimosifolia* are becoming naturalised to a limited extent in suitable localities.

The arrangement of the book is strictly alphabetical, that is, the families are in alphabetical order, as are the genera within each family and also the species within each genus. The full botanical name for each tree comprises three parts: the generic name, the specific name, and the name of the author who first described and named the tree. The name of the author is frequently abbreviated for convenience, for example:

L.   for C. von Linné (C. Linnaeus)
Oliv.   for D. Oliver
DC.   for A. P. De Candolle
Benth. for G. Bentham
Bak. f. for E. G. Baker, or Baker the son
Hutch. for J. Hutchinson

In some instances, immediately under the name of the tree there will be found another name, in italics and in brackets. This is a *synonym*, or a name which was applied to this tree in the past but which is not now considered valid.

The scale of the illustrations

The colour illustrations in this book are reproduced in two sizes; the larger of these represents almost half natural size, while the smaller illustrations represent almost a quarter the natural size of the specimens.

Medicinal and poisonous uses of trees

To the rural African peoples, medicine means far more than the drug to cure a disease; it means also the poison to kill an enemy, the charm carried to ensure a safe journey, and it is also witchcraft and magic with their evil influences. To simple people the world over, folklore, superstition and fear of the unknown are ever present in their daily lives, and it is no different in Africa. There is no doubt that some of the healing properties ascribed to parts of these trees are quite valid, and it has been proved that others are poisonous to a greater or lesser extent. Much has been done to discourage and forbid the use of poisons as such, but there is some evidence that they are still used in the more remote parts of Africa. It is quite certain, however, that much of the healing and many of the cures claimed are due to pure faith, either in the doctor or in the reputation of the 'medicine'. Sometimes the use made of some part of the tree is associated with some property of that tree, so a tree with milky latex might be used to increase lactation, either in domestic animals or in women.

Even with the advance of western medicine and the establishment of dispensaries and clinics in the rural areas, there are many African witch-doctors who still flourish, having set themselves up in peaceful opposition to their modern counterparts, and they get their custom from people who consider that treatment in the

4

hospitals is too slow. Witch-doctors frequently interweave their treatments with mysticism, using a combination of medicine and charms—and this is by no means confined to Africa, either!

The various medicinal uses which are described in this book have been culled from many sources and do not always apply to the Africans of the highveld. We wish to make it clear that we make no claim as to their effectiveness. There is no doubt that some of these medicines are very harmful, and idle experimentation by unqualified persons could prove dangerous.

Vernacular and common names
While some common names are apt and their use well established, many are ambiguous in their application and are frequently a source of confusion; the same name may be applied to different species in different parts of Rhodesia or in different countries. Only the most widely used English or Afrikaans common names have been selected.

With the vernacular names, much the same situation exists; there are several names in different Shona and Ndebele dialects which are used for the same species of tree. Furthermore, many of the names may apply to the genus rather than to the species and may include several species with somewhat similar appearance, and they may even cut across genera and families. As far as possible only one name in each of the two main languages has been included for each tree. This is the one which is considered to be most widely used.

The Shona names are indicated by the letters SH.

The Ndebele names are indicated by the letter N.

Acknowledgements
The coloured illustrations used in this book are taken from the original watercolour paintings by the late Olive H. Coates Palgrave, and they featured in the book *Trees of Central Africa* published by the National Publications Trust in 1956. This book has been out of print for many years now, and we are pleased to be able to bring nearly half of these paintings to a new and wider public in this present volume.

We should like to acknowledge the permission given by the Trustees of the National Museums and Monuments of Rhodesia to make use of the printing blocks which were prepared originally for the colour illustrations in the book *Trees of Central Africa*. This has made possible the production of the fine colour plates which appear in this present publication.

We are extremely grateful to Mr Stephen Mavi for his advice on the selection of the most widely used Shona and Ndebele names.

Finally, we should like to thank Miss Ann Posner, Mrs Hazel Millen and Mrs Sally Milne for so competently handling the typing of the manuscript.

References

Flora Zambesiaca Vols I, II and III, Part 1

Flora of Tropical East Africa

COATES PALGRAVE, *Trees of Central Africa*, National Publications Trust, 1956

GILGES, W., *Some African Poison Plants and Medicines of Northern Rhodesia*, Occasional Paper No. 11, Rhodes-Livingstone Museum, 1955

SYMON, S. A., *African Medicine in the Mankoya District, Northern Rhodesia*, Rhodes-Livingstone Institute, Communications No. 15, 1959

DE WINTER, B., *et al*, *Sixty-six Trees of the Transvaal*, Botanical Research Institute, Pretoria, 1966

CODD, L. E. W., *Trees and Shrubs of the Kruger National Park*, Department of Agriculture, South Africa, 1951

WATT, JOHN MITCHELL, and BREYER-BRANDWIJK, MARIA GERDINA, *The Medicinal and Poisonous Plants of Southern and East Africa*, E. & S. Livingstone, 1962

ANACARDIACEAE (MANGO FAMILY)

1 **LANNEA DISCOLOR** (Sond.) Engl. *Plate 1*

livelong
SH *mushamba, mugan'acha*
N *isigangatsha*

This species occurs from Zaire southwards to the Transvaal. In Rhodesia it is a common tree of the open woodlands of the highveld. It also occurs in *Terminalia sericea* woodland on Kalahari sand, on rocky slopes in *Brachystegia boehmii* woodland and a variety of other similar habitats at lower altitudes.

It is a small to medium sized deciduous tree, usually 4 m to 7 m in height; its maximum size is probably 10 m to 11 m, but this is unusual rather than common. The bark is often reddish grey and smooth, but in older and larger specimens the bark becomes roughish with small corky flakes.

The flowers are sweetly scented and are small and inconspicuous in themselves but are borne in clusters of spikes, up to 13 or 14 cm long, on the tips of the branches. These are produced when the trees are leafless, and are very distinctive. Male and female flowers are separate, the female spikes being shorter and more compact than the male spikes. The flowers appear from July to October. The small fruits, about the size of a pea, develop in October and November.

Poles cut from these trees, and used as fencing standards, strike and grow easily; this has given the tree its popular name, livelong. The wood is soft and light, and is used to make floats for fishing nets, and, in times past, made good brake blocks for wagons. If the bark on a young branchlet is carefully tapped and knocked it can be slipped entirely from the wood, and children use this to make effective pop-guns.

The bark and roots are used medicinally by Africans for a variety of disorders, particularly children's complaints, ranging from fever to constipation.

Three other species of *Lannea* occur in Rhodesia: *L. humilis* is a small tree whose distribution just reaches the extreme north-west of Rhodesia; *L. edulis* is a common shrublet of woodland and vlei margins in the highveld; *L. stuhlmannii* is a sizable tree of lower altitudes, and is particularly common along rivers.

2 OZOROA RETICULATA (Bak. f.) R. & A. Fernandes
(*Heeria reticulata* (Bak. f.) Engl.)   *Plate 2*

heeria, raisin bush, tar berry
SH *mugaragunguwo*
N   *isafice*

This is an extremely poly-morphic species also occur-ring in Zambia, Malawi, Tanzania, Moçambique and South Africa.

It occurs in a wide variety of habitats, open woodland, grassland, on termite mounds and at vlei margins or among granite rocks.

The size is variable, but it is usually a small, deci-duous tree, 3 m to 4 m in height, and 7 m is probably about its maximum. It can remain small and shrubby, sometimes even less than 1 m, in the form of short woody shoots from a rootstock.

8

The flowers are in short, inconspicuous heads; male and female flowers are separate and are produced from November to February.

The fruits are small, oblong, turn black when ripe and are pitted and wrinkled like a raisin; hence the popular name, raisin bush. The fruits, produced from January to April and even later, are eaten eagerly by birds and by humans, too.

The roots of this tree are used medicinally by Africans. In countries north of Rhodesia, an infusion of the roots is used for stomach complaints. It is taken internally for stomach pains and for diarrhoea, when the infusion is drunk frequently for about four hours and then the same infusion is given as an enema, using a small calabash as a syringe. Finally, a powder from the pounded roots is applied to check any external irritation after purging has ceased. Some years ago the African doctor charged a fee of fifty cents for this treatment, but no doubt the price has now risen!

In years past the wood was used by some Africans to make their arrowheads; it was also added to molten iron during smelting as it was claimed that this improved the quality of the metal, making it more malleable.

The specific name *reticulata* refers to the conspicuous net veining, or reticulate veining, on the undersurface of the leaves which are also densely velvety, or furry. The upper surface of the leaves is without hairs and shiny.

The popular name, heeria, is a carry-over from the years when this tree was called *Heeria reticulata*.

Three other species of *Ozoroa* occur in Rhodesia: *O. longepetiolata* is confined to the serpentine-derived soils of the Great Dyke; *O. obovata* has a coastal distribution from Kenya to Natal and only just extends into the Gona-re-Zhou area in the southeast of Rhodesia; *O. paniculosa* occurs in South Africa and Botswana and has been recorded in the south and west of Rhodesia. The distinction between the latter species and *O. reticulata* is not always clear-cut.

APOCYNACEAE (OLEANDER FAMILY)

3 DIPLORHYNCHUS
CONDYLOCARPON (Muell. Arg.) Pich.   *Plate 3*

rubber tree
SH *mutowa*
N   *inkamamasane*

The genus *Diplorhynchus* contains only this one species, which occurs from Zaire and Tanzania southwards through Rhodesia to South West Africa, Botswana and the northern Transvaal.

This is a very common tree in woodland and dry rocky places in the highveld. It is one of the plants which tolerates the serpentine-derived soils of the Great Dyke, and often occurs as a co-dominant with *Combretum zeyheri*. It is also widespread at lower altitudes in a variety of situations.

The size of this tree is variable, often only 4 m to 6 m in height, but much larger specimens, up to 10 m and 12 m, are not unusual. The bark is dark brownish grey, rough, corky and scaly. The leaves are deciduous.

The small flowers, in insignificant heads, appear in October and November.

The fruits are paired capsules, becoming dark brown and woody, each splitting to release two seeds with reddish, papery wings. The fruits are produced from March to May.

This tree contains a milky latex, in common with many members of this family. In this case the latex forms a soft, rubber-like substance and it has been used as a bird-lime to entrap small birds. A pointer to its practical use can be seen in the story which was told by Mr Fred Eyles, one of this country's early and indefatigable botanists. He said that on one occasion he was travelling by car from Salisbury to Bulawayo; this was many years before the fine tarmac road of today and, when he was still some 200 km from Bulawayo, the car struck a rock which cracked the oil sump. Any sort of repair seemed almost impossible, and Mr Eyles left his companions and walked off into the bush where he had noticed a number of these rubber trees growing. As he passed each tree he cut it with a pocket knife and collected some of the latex that ran out. After about an hour he had collected a thick, sticky mass in his hands, and he returned to the car to find the damaged sump no nearer repair, and his companions' tempers more than a little frayed by his long absence. Mr Eyles said, however, that they managed to plug and seal the crack in the sump with his 'rubber', and that this held very satisfactorily all the way to Bulawayo.

The latex is also used by the Nyanja people in eastern Zambia to smear on the hides of their drums, as this improves their quality and tone.

Parts of the tree are used medicinally. In Angola a strong decoction of the root was used, and possibly still is used, by Europeans to relieve blackwater fever. In Zambia Africans use the leaves as a remedy for headaches and stomach disorders. An infusion of the root is used to treat diarrhoea.

The wood has an attractive grain and can be used for ornaments, or for furniture if large enough logs can be obtained. The tree is fire-resistant and will withstand even repeated early burning. Poles cut from these trees make good fencing posts, and they often take root and grow.

There is a superstition in southern Malawi that this tree will prevent rain. The Africans there believe that a man about to make a long journey can ensure a rain-free trip if he drinks nothing just before setting off, and tucks some leaves from this *Diplorhynchus* into his belt. This, they are sure, will safeguard him on his travels.

ARALIACEAE (CABBAGE TREE FAMILY)

4 CUSSONIA KIRKII Seem.

Plate 4

cabbage tree
SH *mufenje*
N   *umelemele*

This tree is widely distributed in tropical Africa from Sierra Leone to Tanzania and south to Rhodesia and Moçambique. There is a possibility that this species will prove to be the same as *C. arborea* A. Rich., a species described from Ethiopia. If this proves to be the case, then *C. kirkii* would fall into synonymy and *C. arborea* would be the valid name. A common tree of *Brachystegia* woodland along the central watershed, this species is partial to rocky situations.

The size varies considerably. As generally seen, the maximum size is probably about 4 m to 8 m, but under ideal conditions it can be larger, and in Zambia can easily reach 13 m. The bark is light brown and corky; the leaves are deciduous.

These are strange looking trees and are quite unmistakable at all times, but especially so in the flowering and fruiting season when the untidy clusters of long spikes look like the tentacles of a frightened octopus. The flowers, in themselves small and insignificant, are carried on long, twisting spikes up to 30 cm long. Six to twelve spikes arise together in terminal heads. The flowers appear from September to November.

The fruits are small, 5 to 6 mm in diameter, rounded and slightly fleshy, becoming purplish when mature. They develop from November to January.

Plate 2 OZOROA RETICULATA, page 8

Plate 1 LANNEA DISCOLOR, page 7

Plate 3 DIPLORHYNCHUS CONDYLOCARPON, page 10

Plate 4 CUSSONIA KIRKII, page 12 (Head of mature leaves and of fruits much reduced in size.)

Plate 5 COMMIPHORA MARLOTHII, page 14

Plate 6 MAYTENUS SENEGALENSIS, page 15

Plate 7 PARINARI CURATELLIFOLIA, page 17

Plate 9 COMBRETUM ZEYHERI, page 22

Plate 8 COMBRETUM MOLLE, page 20

Plate 11 MONOTES GLABER, page 27

Plate 10 TERMINALIA MOLLIS, page 24

Plate 12 TERMINALIA SERICEA, page 25

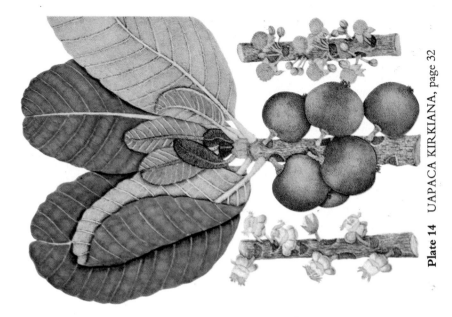

Plate 14 UAPACA KIRKIANA, page 32

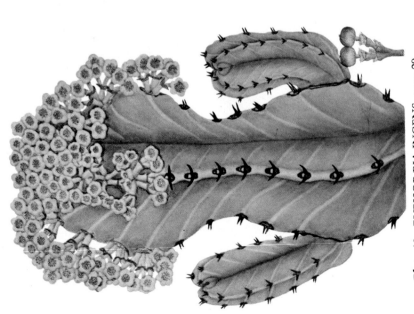

Plate 13 EUPHORBIA INGENS, page 29

The leaves are very large, compound, and more or less completely divided, like the fingers of a hand, into five or more leaflets. The leaf stalk may reach 30 cm long, and the individual leaflets may be as large as 26 cm long by 10 cm broad.

The wood is of little value as timber, but the Africans in Malawi use it to make the keys for their xylophones. These are made from strips of wood carefully cut to size and shaped with a small-bladed axe, or *demo*. These keys are usually about 37 cm long by 2,5 to 4 cm wide, but they may be larger if the musician so desires. Seven keys are used, and their ends are fixed to two pieces of wood which, in turn, are secured to the sounding board. These keys are then struck with a small piece of wood about the size of a pencil. The wood from *Cussonia kirkii* produces very attractive, liquid notes.

5 **COMMIPHORA MARLOTHII** Engl. *Plate 5*

paper-bark
SH *mupepe*
N *umkwazakwaza*

This species also occurs in
Zambia, Botswana and the
Transvaal. It is a common
species of granite kopjes at
most altitudes in Rhodesia
and was originally described
from the Matopos.

Commiphora marlothii is a
medium sized, deciduous
tree, rarely more than 7 m
in height; the trunk is comparatively stout, and can
measure 40 cm in diameter;
it is green and succulent,
with large sheets of thin,
yellowish, papery bark
peeling away from it. The
flowers are in small, inconspicuous heads; the male and female
flowers are separate and are produced in October and November.

The fruits, which are small, round, about the size of a pea and
brownish in colour, appear from November to January.

This tree is known mainly for the paper which peels abundantly
from the thick, rather succulent trunk. The paper itself is rather
brittle and tears easily, but one can write on it if a soft-lead pencil
is used.

There are thirteen other species of *Commiphora* occurring
naturally in Rhodesia: *C. merkeri* and *C. pyracanthoides* with
simple leaves, *C. africana* and *C. schimperi* with trifoliate leaves
and the rest, of which *C. mollis* is the most common and the one
most likely to be found on the highveld, with pinnate leaves.

In general the genus *Commiphora* is characteristic of the hotter,
drier parts of Africa.

6 MAYTENUS SENEGALENSIS (Lam.) Exell   *Plate 6*

confetti bush
SH *chizhuzhu*
N *isihlangu*

This very variable species occurs throughout Africa south of the Sahara from Senegal to South West Africa, Botswana, the Transvaal and Natal. It also occurs in southern Spain and along the African shore of the Mediterranean, through Arabia, as far east as Pakistan and India, turning up again in Aldabra Island and northern Madagascar.

Over its whole range, it is to be found in a wide variety of habitats from sea level to 2 400 m, and is particularly common in the open *Brachystegia* woodland of the Rhodesian highveld. In some areas it is frequently found growing on termitaria.

It is a small, deciduous tree, rarely reaching 7 m in height. The bark is light grey in colour. The branches may be armed with rigid, straight spines.

The sweetly scented flowers are borne in profusion in May and June, but there can be a second flowering season, from about August to September.

The fruits are small capsules, 6 to 7 mm long by 5 to 6 mm wide, reddish brown when mature, splitting to release two to four seeds. They develop in September to October following a May to June flowering, or in December to January after a spring flowering season.

This small tree is a beautiful sight when covered with its profusion of white flowers. These are only short-lived and do not stay
on the tree for long, falling when they still appear quite fresh.
The fallen flowers can be gathered by the handful and this gives
the tree its common name, confetti bush.

The wood is yellowy white, hard, straight-grained and durable,
but the pieces of timber are usually so small that there is little use
for them; it is possible that it could provide a useful boxwood.
The spines are used to stretch the hide in the covering of African
drums.

Parts of this tree are used in African medicine. In Zambia the
roots are chipped into small pieces and placed in beer, and then
this is drunk as an aphrodisiac; in the north-western areas of that
country the plant is used as a snake bite remedy. Ideally, the head
of the snake is burnt with the roots of this tree, then the resulting
ash is mixed to a paste with oil and placed on the bites themselves,
and also on the patient's tongue. If it is impossible to carry out
this whole procedure, then an infusion of the leaves is given to
the victim to drink. In the Transvaal the roots are boiled and then
applied as a poultice for pains in the ribs; first the poultice is
placed on the opposite side of the chest from the pain, and then
one is put over the painful area itself. At the same time the liquid
from the boiled roots is made into a porridge with mealie meal,
and this is given to the patient to eat. The roots are also used to
cure haemoptysis, which is the spitting or coughing up of blood.

Further afield, in India, the powdered bark is mixed to a paste
with mustard oil, and this is rubbed onto the head to get rid of lice.

There are nine other species of *Maytenus* in Rhodesia, of which
the two most widespread are *M. heterophylla* and *M. undata*. The
latter is easily distinguished from *M. senegalensis* by its tightly
clustered flowers, and the flower stalks are not branched.
M. heterophylla, however, is extremely variable and is so closely
allied to *M. senegalensis* that the two are often confused.

The points to look for in separating them are:

M. heterophylla:
(a) The shoots are greenish, and are usually angular or lined.
(b) The fruits have three compartments and are yellow to red.
(c) The leaves are plain green, with acutely toothed margins.

M. senegalensis:
(a) The shoots are reddish, and are not angular or lined.

(b) The fruits have two compartments and are reddish brown.

(c) The leaves are conspicuously glaucous; that is, they have a marked greyish or bluish bloom.

There is no doubt, however, that these features merge and overlap, and it remains very difficult to tell these two species apart; the only really diagnostic feature is the colour of the leaves —the greyish blue bloom in *M. senegalensis* which is absent in *M. heterophylla*.

CHRYSOBALANACEAE

7 **PARINARI CURATELLIFOLIA** Planch. ex Benth.
(*Parinari mobola* Oliv.) *Plate 7*

hissing tree, mobola plum
SH *muhacha*
N *umkhuna*

This species occurs from Senegal to the Sudan and southwards through Rhodesia to the Transvaal and Natal. It has been divided into two subspecies, subsp. *curatellifolia* and subsp. *mobola*, because of differences in the covering of the leaves, the venation of the leaves and their texture. The two subspecies are not always readily distinguishable and many specimens are found with intermediate characters. All the specimens occurring in Rhodesia are probably referable to subsp. *mobola*.

It is most characteristic as a scattered tree in grassland on sandy soil where there is a high water table. It also occurs on the margin of *Brachystegia-Julbernardia* woodland and on granite kopjes, but its occurrence is probably always dependent on a good water supply. For this reason it is sometimes considered to be an indicator of a high water table and poor drainage.

It is a large, evergreen, spreading tree, typically mushroom shaped, usually up to 12 m in height in Rhodesia, but it can reach twice this height in more northerly countries. The bark is dark grey in colour.

The small, insignificant white flowers are produced in short, rusty coloured, furry heads from July to October.

The fruits, about the size of a plum, are borne in profusion from January to March, though they may be found on the trees much later than this. The flowering and fruiting seasons vary somewhat in different localities and under different conditions; for example, in Zambia the main fruiting season is in October and November.

The fruits are edible and when ripe the yellow flesh is delicious, though a little dry; this surrounds a single large seed. The fruit forms an important part of the diet of the African people, and the trees are greatly valued; in the western areas of Zambia, at least, these trees have been declared reserved fruit trees. Also, in his *Goldfields Diaries*, Thomas Baines recorded that elephants are very fond of these fruits.

The beautiful, shady trees form a conspicuous feature of the landscape, and it is easy to understand that one of them was chosen to bear the final tribute to Dr David Livingstone. Dr Livingstone died in 1873 at Chitambo's Village in central Zambia, and the commemorative inscription was carved by Jacob Wainwright on the trunk of a fine specimen of *Parinari curatellifolia*:

Dr Livingstone
May 4th, 1873
Chuma, Souza, Mniasere
Vchopere

No part of the fruit is wasted. The flesh is eaten, sometimes made into a porridge, or a refreshing, non-alcoholic drink, or a highly esteemed syrup. This is prepared by mixing the flesh with water, allowing it to stand for several days, then drawing off the liquid and slowly boiling this down until it becomes a thick syrup. A highly intoxicating drink is also prepared from the fruits, but the recipe for this has not been divulged.

The roots of the tree feature in African medicine. For a discharging ear the African doctor prepares drops by soaking the roots in cold water for an hour. He then pours a little of this liquid into the ear four times a day for about two weeks, using a spoon or a cupped leaf. An alternative to these drops is the rendered down fat from a python; not any snake will do, it must be a python. The fee for either of these treatments varies from $1,50 to $2.

The liquid obtained by boiling pieces of the bark in water for two minutes is used as a hot fomentation on the chest in cases of pneumonia.

This is quite widely known as the hissing tree; there is a belief that as the tree is chopped it hisses. We have set out to prove this, but have not heard any hissing sound. The wood, however, contains silica crystals which tend to make it gritty, and it is possible that these might cause a slight hiss as the axe blade bites into the trunk.

The light brown, very hard wood is borer-proof and fire-resistant, but is not durable if left exposed to the weather. The silica crystals already mentioned make working the wood very difficult, and saw-blades are rapidly blunted. It has been used fairly extensively, however, for rafters, beams and poles, and for benches. Africans use the wood to make mortars, and they cut their dug-out canoes from the logs.

An infusion of the bark is used in tanning hides and it gives a dark brown colour to the finished skin. The bark is pounded with a little water, and this liquid is rubbed well into the skin as a final dressing.

It has been reported by numerous people that these trees have an unpleasant smell, but it is difficult to say what may cause it.

The only other species of *Parinari* growing in Rhodesia is *Parinari capensis*, the sand apple, which is common in sandy areas. It is a creeping shrub only a few centimetres in height and grows in colonies; its leaves are remarkably similar to those of *Parinari curatellifolia.*

COMBRETACEAE (COMBRETUM FAMILY)

8 **COMBRETUM MOLLE** R.Br. ex Don   *Plate 8*

soft-leaved combretum
SH   *mupembere*
N   *umbondo*

This species occurs throughout tropical Africa, in areas where woodland and wooded grasslands predominate, and extends southwards to South West Africa, Botswana, the Transvaal and Natal. It also occurs in Arabia.

It is one of the most common constituents of the *Brachystegia-Julbernardia* woodlands on the Rhodesian highveld. It is a deciduous, shapely tree reaching 10 m in height, with a brownish grey trunk.

The leaves of this tree are distinctive, soft and velvety. The undersurface of the leaf is densely furry and is conspicuously net veined.

The flowers, small and inconspicuous in themselves, form short, compact, sweetly scented spikes, 3 to 4 cm in length. They appear in profusion from August to October, and are eagerly sought by insects of many types which descend in hordes on a tree in full flower.

The fruits, 1,5 cm to 2,2 cm long, have the typical *combretum* four wings, the wings being reddish brown to brown, rigid and brittle. The fruits mature from March to July.

The leaves and roots are used in African medicine. Fresh leaves, or moistened dry leaves, are used as a dressing for wounds. The inner part of the root, powdered, is used in the same way, and an extract of the roots is used as a cough remedy.

The wood is of good quality, is termite-proof and borer-proof and is quite widely used by farmers for fencing posts and for general farm use.

Besides the two species illustrated in this book, there are seventeen other species of *Combretum* occurring in Rhodesia, ranging from the dwarf *C. platypetalum* (redwings) through the climbing, spectacular red-flowered species *C. microphyllum* and *C. paniculatum* (the burning bush), to large trees like *C. imberbe* (leadwood) and *C. collinum*.

9 **COMBRETUM ZEYHERI** Sond.

Plate 9

large-fruited combretum
SH *muruka*
N *umbondo*

This species occurs from Zaire and Tanzania southwards to South West Africa, Botswana, the Transvaal and Natal. It occurs in woodland and wooded grassland. It is very tolerant of soils with a high metal or serpentine content and, with *Diplorhynchus condylocarpon*, is a common tree on the grass covered hills of the Great Dyke.

It is usually a slender, deciduous tree, reaching heights of 12 to 13 m. The bark is brownish grey in colour, smoothish, with patches of small flakes.

The leaves are larger, darker green and less hairy than *C. molle*. The upper surface is smooth; the lower, grey and finely furry.

The flowers, in short spikes, are insignificant, rather resembling mignonette. They appear from August to November.

The fruits, typically four-winged, are large, from 5 cm to 7,5 cm in length. They are light yellowish brown when ripe, and develop from April to August.

The leaves, roots and bark of *C. zeyheri* are used medicinally. The smoke from burning dried leaves is inhaled to relieve coughs. The dried leaves are used to cure colic. They are powdered and soaked in water for thirty minutes and a cupful of this is then sipped slowly, when relief from the pain is expected. The liquid is very bitter, and it is not often that the patient takes more than one cupful.

Among the Mankoya people in Zambia, the leaves and bark of *C. zeyheri*, together with the roots of cassava, feature in their cure of smallpox. The treatment is divided into three parts: an enema, eyedrops and an ointment.

(a) The enema. This is applied using a small calabash as a syringe, and the liquid is prepared by pounding the leaves of C. zeyheri and then warming these in water.

(b) The eyedrops. These are prepared by soaking the cassava roots in water for ten minutes. This liquid is then strained and a few drops are put into each eye four times a day for about a week.

(c) The ointment. The inner bark of C. zeyheri is stamped and pounded, a little water continually being added until a paste is formed. The smallpox pustules are then pricked with a splinter of wood and the ointment is smeared onto them. This is used only once.

Throughout this treatment the patient has to lie on a bed of earth made from a particular type of small termite nest. The fee for this treatment is usually about $2.

The roots, together with those of the tree violet, *Securidaca longepedunculata*, and the blood-like sap of the mukwa, *Pterocarpus angolensis*, are used in the treatment of nose bleeding. The pounded roots, mixed to a paste with fat, are used also as an ointment to relieve haemorrhoids.

The wood is yellow in colour, termite-proof and borer-proof, and is a useful general purpose timber. The roots also yield a fibre which is used for making baskets and trays.

C. zeyheri is readily distinguished from the other Rhodesian species by the large, yellowish green to pale brown fruit. The style frequently protrudes in a characteristic fashion from the flower bud.

large-fruited terminalia
SH   *mususu-mukuru*
N   *umangwe-omkulu*

This species occurs in west tropical Africa, Zaire and east tropical Africa and reaches its southern limit in Angola, Zambia and Rhodesia.

It is a tree of woodland and wooded grassland and often occurs in the transition zone between vlei and woodland.

It is a large, deciduous tree, reaching 12 to 13 m in height. The bark is brownish grey and corky, with longitudinal fissures. The branchlets, too, are corky.

The flowers are small, insignificant, borne in spikes up to 15 cm long, and appear from October to December.

The fruits, typical of all the *Terminalia* species, have a rigid, brittle wing completely encircling the seed. These fruits are pale, brownish green, and up to 9,5 cm in length. When the leaves fall, these fruits, hanging on the tree in heavy clusters, are most distinctive; they mature from January to April.

This is one of the few species of *Terminalia* which does not produce beautiful red, pinkish or purple fruits. In this species the fruits mature to a brownish colour, which may be lightly touched with pink, but no more than that.

The wood is yellow, very hard, termite-proof and lasts for years in the ground. It does not burn well and is easy to saw and turn, but difficult to split. It has been used for the spokes of wheels and as survey poles.

T. stenostachya is distinguished by its non-corky branchlets and usually much smaller fruits and narrower leaves. It is, however, a very closely allied species and is thought to hybridise with *T. mollis*. It has been suggested that all supposed Rhodesian material of *T. mollis* is of hybrid origin, but this seems unlikely.

Besides *T. stenostachya*, *T. sericea* and *T. mollis*, there are seven other species of *Terminalia* occurring in Rhodesia.

11 TERMINALIA SERICEA Burch. ex DC.　　*Plate 12*

mangwe
SH *mususu*
N *umangwe*

This species is also common in South West Africa, Botswana and the Transvaal and reaches its northern limits in Zaire and Tanzania.

It occurs in *Combretum-Terminalia* and *Colophospermum* woodland, and wooded grassland of the lower altitudes where it is frequently dominant or co-dominant. It also occurs in wooded grassland on the highveld, but never becomes a major component of the vegetation under these conditions.

It is usually a medium sized, deciduous tree, about 8 to 9 m in height; under ideal conditions it can double this size, but this is rare in Rhodesia. The bark is rough, fissured and dark brownish grey in colour.

The flowers are small, whitish, and form a short spike about 5 cm long. They appear on the trees from July to January.

The typical *Terminalia* fruits are rather small, 2,5 to 3 cm long, and become a very attractive rose pink colour when they mature between January and July.

The leaves of this tree are beautiful and the early pioneers, travelling through the Mangwe Pass, thought that this was the famous silver-leaf tree of the Cape Peninsula (*Leucadendron argenteum*; family *Proteaceae*). The leaves of *Terminalia sericea* do not approach the spectacular beauty of the leaves of the silver tree, but they are also covered with silvery, silky hairs. In fact, the specific name *sericea* means silky.

The roots of this tree are used in African medicine. A decoction of the roots, which is very bitter to taste, is swallowed to stop diarrhoea and to relieve colic pains. It is also used as an eyewash for certain diseases of the eyes. The outer layers of the roots, boiled in water, provide a liquid which is used as a hot fomentation to relieve pneumonia.

An extract of the bark is used in tanning, as a final dressing, and gives a yellow colour to the finished hide.

The wood is yellow and hard, as is the case with most of the *Terminalia* species. It provides a very useful general purpose wood, and has been used for making furniture. Posts cut from these trees will stand in the ground for years.

DIPTEROCARPACEAE

12 **MONOTES GLABER** Sprague *Plate* 11

SH *mushava*
N *inyunya*

The *Dipterocarpaceae* is a family confined to the tropics of the Old World and is not represented in South Africa. *Monotes glaber* has a limited distribution in western and southern Zambia, northern Botswana and Rhodesia.

In Rhodesia it is a common constituent of *Brachystegia-Julbernardia* woodland. It is sometimes dominant in vlei margins.

It is a small to medium sized, deciduous tree, normally reaching a maximum height of about 10 m. Under certain conditions it may be larger than this, sometimes even considerably larger. The bark is roughish, and a brown grey in colour. The smooth, glossy leaves are a very characteristic yellow green, which give a typical, almost brown look to the whole tree.

The flowers are small and not conspicuous, and are produced from November to February. The fruits are often mistaken for flowers. The sepals are persistent and grow with the fruit; they are at first yellowish green touched with pink, but later become light brown, hard and brittle. These large, persistent sepals look very much like papery petals, and they seem to form a flower many times larger than the original; these are sometimes used by florists in dry arrangements. The fruit itself, inside these papery sepals, is a nut about the size of a pea. The mature fruits can be found from February to July.

The leaves are sometimes used in African medicine in the treatment of burns. They are collected, dried, and crushed to a powder; this is then mixed with the juice from a grass to form a paste. This ointment is smeared over the burns which it is hoped to cure in four days.

The tree is very resistant to fire, and is one of the most termite-resistant of all indigenous woods. It is also very durable and easy to work, having a straight grain, but it does not nail well. It has been used to make permanent posts and rafters and, if large enough logs were available, could also be used for making furniture.

Two other species of *Monotes* occur in Rhodesia: *M. katangensis* reaches its southern limit in the Zambezi valley and *M. engleri*, bearing leaves with greyish, silvery hairs beneath, is widespread in woodland at medium altitudes.

Plate 15 PSEUDOLACHNOSTYLIS MAPROUNEIFOLIA, page 31

Plate 17   BRACHYSTEGIA BOEHMII, page 35

Plate 16   BAUHINIA PETERSIANA, page 34

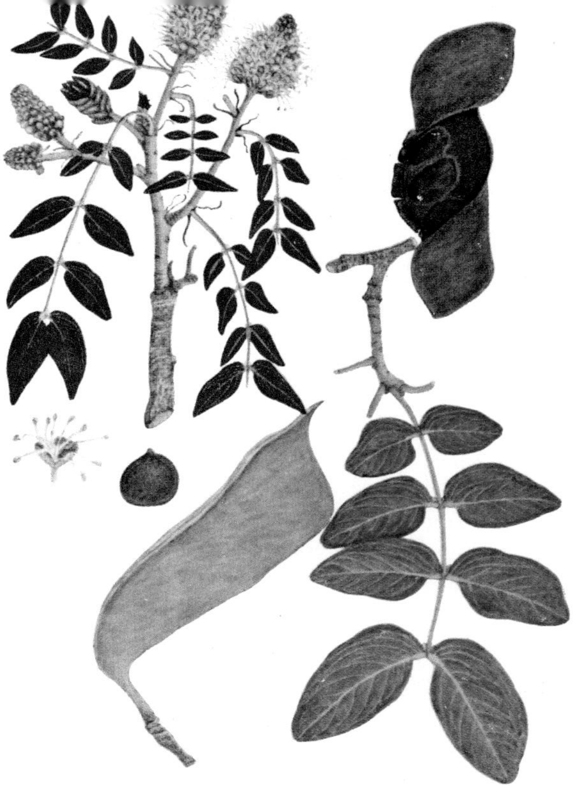

Plate 19 BRACHYSTEGIA SPICIFORMIS, page 38

Plate 18 BRACHYSTEGIA GLAUCESCENS, page 37

Plate 20 CASSIA ABBREVIATA, page 40

Plate 22 PILIOSTIGMA THONNINGII, page 45

Plate 21 JULBERNARDIA GLOBIFLORA, page 42

Plate 23 PELTOPHORUM AFRICANUM, page 44

Plate 25 ACACIA KARROO, page 47

Plate 24 SCHOTIA BRACHYPETALA, page 46

Plate 26 ACACIA POLYACANTHA, page 49

Plate 27 ACACIA SIEBERANA, page 50

EUPHORBIACEAE (EUPHORBIA FAMILY)

13 **EUPHORBIA INGENS** E. Mey. ex Boiss.   *Plate* 13

candelabra tree
SH *mukonde*
N *umhlonhlo*

This tree, which forms such a striking feature of the Rhodesian landscape, is widespread in tropical Africa and extends as far south as the Transvaal and Natal. It occurs most frequently on rocky kopjes and termite mounds.

This strangely formed tree can reach quite a considerable size, sometimes 10 to 11 m or more. The ascending branches, with paired spines up to 1,5 cm long over almost their whole length, are soft and brittle, breaking easily to release copious milky latex.

This tree is a xerophyte; that is, it is fully adapted to growth under very dry conditions and the structure of the whole tree is geared to conserving water. In order to reduce water loss by transpiration, leaves are absent. To compensate for this the stem has developed four or five flanges, thus increasing the green surface area, so that the stem has taken over the vital process of photosynthesis which is normally carried out by the leaves.

The flowers are green and fleshy and appear in April. The fruits are round, about the size of a pea, and mature in August.

Many people refer to this tree and other *Euphorbia* species as cacti. This is not correct, for a true cactus contains clear, watery sap while all the *Euphorbia* species contain a thick, sticky, milky latex. There is only one true member of the family *Cactaceae* which is indigenous to Africa; this is *Rhipsalis baccifera* which is a strange little plant, living as an epiphyte on the great trees of some of the evergreen forests. It occurs in Rhodesia in some of the forest areas along the eastern border. All the cacti seen in gardens have been introduced, mostly from Central America.

The latex from *E. ingens* becomes very sticky when allowed to dry partially in the air, and it has been used as bird-lime to snare small birds which become stuck in it.

This latex is very toxic and can cause intense irritation and even blistering of the skin. Cattle which have been driven through dense bush where numbers of these trees are growing may get severe burns around the eyes, lips and on the face, and cases have been so severe that the unfortunate beasts have had to be destroyed.

Africans in the Limpopo valley use the latex as a fish poison; they soak a bundle of grass in half a cup of latex, then tie the sodden grass to a stone and throw this into the pool. Dr Watt states that he has seen fish rising to the surface some fifteen minutes later, apparently paralysed but still breathing.

A single drop of the latex in the eye causes intense pain and temporary blindness, blistering the eyeball and the cornea, and in extreme cases may end in the loss of the eye.

Despite this dramatic history, the latex is still used in African medicine, in very small doses, as a drastic purgative, as a cure for dipsomania and as a treatment for cancer. There seems to be no doubt that the doctor, and the patient, run a very grave risk; there have been several recorded deaths from an accidental overdose. It is easy to see its use as an instrument for murder; before death the unfortunate person experiences vomiting, violent abdominal pains and excessive and intractable purging.

The flowers of several species of *Euphorbia*, including *E. ingens*, produce quantities of nectar, which is collected by bees and produces 'noors honey'. This cannot be eaten, as it contains an irritant which is carried across from the flowers and causes a hot, burning feeling in the mouth, which is only made worse by drinking water.

There are some forty-eight other Rhodesian species of *Euphorbia* varying in habit from low-growing garden weeds like *E. prostrata* and *E. inaequilatera* to spiny, succulent trees like *E. cooperi* and *E. confinalis*.

14 PSEUDOLACHNOSTYLIS MAPROUNEIFOLIA Pax

Plate 15

duikerberry
SH *mukuvazviyo, mutsonzowa*
N *umqhobampunzi*

This tree occurs as far north as Zaire and Tanzania and as far south as South West Africa, Botswana and the Transvaal. In Rhodesia it is frequent in woodland and wooded grassland in the highveld of the central watershed, and also occurs in different types of woodland at lower altitudes.

It is a medium sized, deciduous tree, 7 m to 10 m in height. The bark is light grey brown in colour. The flowers are small, insignificant, greenish white, and appear from July to November.

The fruits are round and berry-like, up to 2 cm in diameter, and turn pale yellow when ripe. They develop from May onwards, but remain on the tree for a long time and there may be overlapping between the seasons, so that new young fruits appear before the old ones have fallen. The ripe fruits are eaten by antelopes; this has given the tree its popular name, duikerberry.

The great beauty of this tree lies in the spectacular, fiery colours of the leaves in autumn. At all times it is an attractive tree, with light green leaves, but in autumn and winter it is splendid.

In parts of Zambia the Africans use the milky latex, taking it internally and also inhaling the smoke from burning roots, to treat pneumonia. A bark extract is used to relieve diarrhoea.

The trees are fire-resistant, but they respond well if protected, becoming very shapely, with good crowns and straight boles.

The smooth, even-grained, moderately heavy wood is used in toy-making, turnery and handicrafts.

Superstition surrounds this tree in the central and southern provinces of Malawi, and people there believe that the tree harbours a spirit. Women going out into the fields to harvest the crops must placate the 'msolo' spirit, so they lay a small offering of a few bunches of grain at the foot of the tree. If none of these trees happens to grow anywhere near, then the women must choose a substitute and place their offering at the foot of some other tree; this, they say, is quite in order, for the 'msolo' will accept the gesture and understand their difficulties.

Only one species of *Pseudolachnostylis* occurs in Rhodesia.

15 UAPACA KIRKIANA Muell. Arg.   *Plate 14*

mahobohobo, wild loquat
SH   *muzhanje*
N   *umhobohobo*

This is a distinctive tree, unmistakable in appearance, which occurs as far north as central Tanzania, then southwards through Zambia to Angola, Rhodesia and Moçambique. It has not been recorded from South Africa.

It is a common, deciduous woodland tree in Rhodesia, 5 to 6 m in height, at medium altitudes, and is sometimes locally dominant on gravelly soils. It is frost-tender and cannot survive in frost hollows. The young shoots are protected to some extent by the large, curved, coarse leaves which are grouped near the tips of the branches. The bark is rough and dark grey in colour.

The male and female flowers are separate; they are not particularly distinctive and appear from January to April.

The fruits are round, rusty yellow, and about the size of a plum. The skin is quite hard and surrounds sweet, edible flesh containing several large seeds. The fruits mature in June and July. They are delicious to eat and, if allowed to ferment, can be used to make a very pleasant wine. In western Zambia it has been declared a protected food tree.

The liquid obtained by soaking the roots in water for about fifteen minutes is used as a cure for indigestion, and it is said to be especially effective in relieving the very acute pains which apparently follow a gluttonous meal of maize, pumpkins and groundnuts.

Hunters in this country declare that mahobohobo woodland is the very worst in which to hunt, as the brittle dry leaves form a crackling carpet which betrays their every move. Many a frustrated hunter has bitterly declared that the mahobohobo is worse even than the 'Go-away' bird, the Grey Loerie.

Thomas Baines, in his *Goldfields Diaries*, mentioned these trees often, and once made reference to the tree as a means of telling the age of elephant tracks. On one particular occasion he was on the trail of a herd of elephant, 'finding here and there leaves and branches plucked and half-chewed two to three hours ago, and dung, perhaps not more than cold and not yet dry. The large rustling leaf of the makobakoba (a name expressive of the noise it makes) affords the best time test, for in two or three hours it loses its cool, glossy green and begins to look dry and pale.'

The wood is a red brown colour and is reasonably durable, termite-proof and borer-proof. It is medium weight, works fairly easily and polishes well. It is useful as a general purpose wood and provides good charcoal.

Three other species of *Uapaca* are found in Rhodesia: *U. sansibarica* occurs in woodland on hillsides in high rainfall areas in the eastern regions of the country and *U. nitida* in *Brachystegia* woodland at rather lower altitudes in the northern, central and eastern areas; the third is a rare species, as yet undescribed, with stilt roots and occurs in low altitude forests in the Eastern Districts.

LEGUMINOSAE (POD-BEARING FAMILY)
CAESALPINIOIDEAE (CASSIA SUBFAMILY)

16 **BAUHINIA PETERSIANA** Bolle   *Plate 16*

white bauhinia
SH   *mun'ando*
N   *imondo*

This species extends from Zaire and Tanzania to Moçambique and Rhodesia. It is common in woodland and wooded grassland at medium to low altitudes.

It is most often a small evergreen tree 4 m to 5 m in height, though it sometimes forms a spreading bush and it also has a tendency to climb. The bark is powdery and grey brown in colour.

The leaves are typical of *Bauhinia*: simple and deeply divided to give the two 'butterfly wings'. The name *Bauhinia* is linked with these leaves, as the genus was named for the two brothers John and Caspar Bauhin, famous botanists in the sixteenth century.

The leaves are used in a very generally known African remedy for the common cold. The leaves are boiled in water and the steam is inhaled; then the liquid is allowed to cool, and it is drunk.

Thomas Baines, in his *Goldfields Diaries*, wrote that on his journey to the Zambezi in 1863, he and his companions collected the seeds of this tree and, by roasting them and grinding them to a powder, used them as a substitute for coffee. Because of this, the tree was known to early hunters and explorers as the Zambezi coffee.

Three other species of *Bauhinia* occur in Rhodesia. *B. macrantha* is a white-flowered shrub more or less confined to areas of Kalahari sand, *B. galpinii* is a red-flowered, climbing shrub widespread over the country except in the west, and *B. tomentosa* is a yellow-flowered shrub or small tree occurring at low altitudes.

17 BRACHYSTEGIA BOEHMII Taub.   *Plate 17*

mufuti
SH *mupfuti*
N *itshabela*

This species occurs from Zaire and Tanzania southwards to Angola, Botswana, Rhodesia and Moçambique.

It is a common tree of the highveld woodland, frequently locally dominant, particularly on poorly drained soils, and often growing in association with *Julbernardia globiflora* and *Brachystegia spiciformis*.

It is a beautiful, deciduous tree reaching a height of 13 m. The bark is rough and grey in colour.

The flowers are small, insignificant, sweetly scented and grouped together in short, compact spikes which appear from September to December.

The fruits are pods and similar to those of many members of this sub-family. They split explosively, throwing the seeds far from the parent tree. The dark brown pods, 13 to 14 cm long, mature from May to July.

The bark contains three per cent tannin, and an extract is used in tanning hides, as the final dressing, which gives a red brown colour to the finished product. It also provides the best bark rope which Africans use for almost anything requiring durability. The rope is made by stripping off the inner bark in long, narrow lengths, which are then chewed and rolled alternately until they are soft and pliable and so form an excellent cord.

This is one of the four main trees which together produce the spectacular display of coloured foliage in spring in Rhodesia. The freshly burst leaf buds resemble the Prince of Wales feathers, and this name was applied to the tree at one time.

18 **BRACHYSTEGIA GLAUCESCENS** Burtt Davy & Hutch.   *Plate* 18
(*B. tamarindoides* auct.)

mountain acacia
SH   *muunze*
N   *umbuze*

This handsome species has a limited distribution and has been recorded only in Zambia, Moçambique and Rhodesia.

It occurs on rocky slopes and hilltops and is locally dominant and common in these situations in the high-veld in Rhodesia.

It is a large and beautiful tree reaching 15 m in height. The bark is smooth and pale grey in colour. The flowers are incon-spicuous, sweetly scented, borne in short, compact spikes and appear in Sep-

tember and October. The fruit is a large, woody, dark brown pod which matures from April to June.

Brachystegia is a difficult genus to classify, as most of the species hybridise readily with one another and, apart from this, there is considerable variation within each species under different condi-tions of rainfall and altitude. This is also one of the spectacular trees in the spring flush of new foliage.

The wood is liable to borer attack if untreated, but after treat-ment it is useful as a general purpose wood, the red brown heart-wood particularly being of considerable durability. It has been used as a mining timber, in building construction, for flooring joists and for lintels. Some of this wood was used in the early homes of Salisbury and was still in a good state of preservation after fifty years.

msasa
SH   *musasa*
N   *igonde*

This is the most widespread species of *Brachystegia* and occurs from Kenya southwards to Angola, Zambia, Rhodesia, Malawi and Moçambique.

It is dominant over large areas of its range. It often hybridises with other species of *Brachystegia*, and intermediates between *B. microphylla*, *B. glaucescens* and *B. boehmii* are not uncommon in Rhodesia. It is a remarkable fact that none of the species of *Brachystegia*, such an ecologically important genus in Rhodesia, has been recorded from South Africa.

It can grow into a handsome, deciduous tree, reaching a height of 15 m. The bark is rough and grey. The small, insignificant, but sweetly scented flowers form a short, compact spike and appear from August to November. The fruit, a large woody, dark brown pod, matures from May to August.

The bark is astringent, containing thirteen per cent tannin, and

Africans use an extract of this, made by pounding pieces of bark in a little water, in tanning hides; it is used as a final dressing and gives the skin a reddish colour. An infusion of the roots is used to treat dysentery and diarrhoea, and a decoction is used as an eyewash in cases of conjunctivitis.

The msasa is one of the best known of all Rhodesian trees, and is one of the major contributors to the splendid colour display in spring with its flush of young leaves between late August and October. Other countries in the world make great tourist capital out of some particularly beautiful season of the year, for example, 'Holland in tulip time' and 'Japan in cherry blossom time'; it is difficult to believe that these could be any more of a natural spectacle than 'Rhodesia in msasa time'.

These are fine shade trees which are being increasingly cultivated, and not before time. It is very gratifying to see that msasas on a piece of land are now considered a valuable asset. They grow easily from seed, are not easy to transplant and are rather slow-growing.

The wood is brown in colour, coarse and not durable if untreated; it is excellent as a firewood and forms good charcoal. It can be treated, however, which improves its qualities and it can be used as a useful but rather inferior general purpose timber. Its value, however, does not lie in the purely utilitarian properties of its timber; it is an ornamental tree, and one of the most beautiful in the world. It is a handsome tree at all times, and in its season blazes with spectacular beauty.

Besides the three species of *Brachystegia* described in this book, there are four other species which occur in Rhodesia. These are *B. microphylla*, *B. utilis*, *B. manga*, and *B. allenii*, all of which are better known in countries to the north of Rhodesia, and reach the southern-most limit of their range in Rhodesia, only just crossing our borders in the north or east of the country.

long-pod cassia
SH *muremberembe, muvheneka*
N *isihaqa*

This species occurs from
Somalia, Kenya and Zaire
southwards to South West
Africa, Botswana, the
Transvaal and Rhodesia.

The species has been sub-
divided into three sub-
species, two of which,
subsp. *abbreviata* and subsp.
beareana, occur in Rho-
desia. Of these two, subsp.
beareana is the more widespread and the more likely
to be encountered. The difference between the two
lies in the hairiness and the
type of hairs on the undersurface of the leaflets:
subsp. *beareana* has very fine, straight hairs pressed flat against the
surface of the leaflet, while subsp. *abbreviata* has loose, sometimes
curly hairs. Often it is not easy to see this difference with the
naked eye. In all other respects the two subspecies are identical.

This species occurs in woodland and wooded grassland at
medium to low altitudes. It is often found growing on termite
mounds, too.

It is a small to medium sized, deciduous tree, usually 5 m to
7 m in height. The bark is grey or grey brown in colour. The
flowers are beautiful, appearing in large, loose sprays from
September to November. The fruit is a long, narrow, cylindrical
pod, velvety brown in colour, and very conspicuous, measuring
up to 75 cm long. The extraordinarily long pods mature from
December to March.

Various parts of the tree feature in African medicine. The seeds
are sucked as a tonic, the roots are used to relieve severe cases of

abdominal pains and to relieve toothache, and the smoke from a burning twig is inhaled to cure headaches.

One aspect of the medicinal properties of this tree has been substantiated. The subspecies *beareana* was named for Dr O'Sullivan Beare who, in 1902, noted that the Africans used a decoction of the roots to cure blackwater fever. He tried this remedy himself and found that the effects were beneficial. Dr Beare was then instrumental in having a fluid extract from the roots prepared commercially and placed on the market under the name *Cassia beareana*. Since then this has been used from time to time by medical men for the treatment of blackwater fever, with apparently beneficial results. The extract is said to be cardiotonic, diuretic and diaphoretic.

Some twenty-four other species of *Cassia* are indigenous to, or have become naturalised in, Rhodesia but, apart from *C. abbreviata*, only *C. singueana* and *C. petersiana* are trees. Several exotic species of *Cassia* are cultivated as ornamental trees.

21 **JULBERNARDIA GLOBIFLORA** (Benth.) Troupin
(*Isoberlinia globiflora* (Benth.) Hutch. ex Greenway) *Plate* 21

mnondo
SH *munhondo*
N *umshonkwe*

This ecologically important species occurs in Tanzania and Zaire and southwards to Angola, Botswana, Rhodesia and Moçambique. This is perhaps the most common and most widespread tree in Rhodesia. It is often dominant or co-dominant with *Brachystegia spiciformis*, forming the woodlands along the central watershed; it is also widespread in other parts of the country.

It is a handsome, deciduous tree reaching 16 m in height. The bark is rough and grey in colour. The flowers are inconspicuous, forming short, loose heads. They appear from January to May and drop soon after opening. The fruits are large, dark brown, velvety pods, up to 12 cm long and mature from May onwards even into November.

With *Brachystegia spiciformis*, *B. glaucescens* and *B. boehmii*, this tree helps to provide a fine display of colour in the Rhodesian spring. It is often confused with *B. spiciformis*, but there are very clear differences between the two. The flush colours of *Julbernardia* are usually soft pinks and fawns, not the intense reds produced by the species of *Brachystegia*; mnondo bears its pods on the top of the tree, well above the foliage, like a crown, while msasa bears its pods among the leaves; the pods of mnondo are velvety, those of msasa are without hairs; the leaves of mnondo usually have about six pairs of leaflets, and the longest is usually the third or fourth pair, while msasa usually has only about four pairs of leaflets, and the largest is the terminal pair; and finally the leaflets of mnondo are oblong in shape, while those of msasa are rhomboid. The flowering times of the two are also very different.

The wood is hard, coarse and uneven but very durable. It is difficult to work, tending to tear, and it splits badly when nailed. Nevertheless it has been used quite widely as a fairly useful general purpose wood.

The bark rope from this tree is inferior to that obtained from the species of *Brachystegia*, but it is nevertheless useful for ropes, beehives, stitched canoes, cornbins and sacks. The wood has been used for mortars and also for canoes.

There are about eight species of *Julbernardia* and they are all confined to tropical Africa; *J. globiflora* is the only species which occurs in Rhodesia.

peltophorum
SH *muzeze*
N *umsehla*

This handsome tree occurs northwards to Zaire, Zambia, Malawi and Moçambique, and southwards to South West Africa, Botswana, the Transvaal, Swaziland and Natal.

It commonly occurs in wooded grassland and at the margins of vleis; it is also found at lower altitudes. It is a spreading, shapely, deciduous tree, about 7 m to 8 m in height. The bark is brown in colour.

The flowers are very decorative, in heavy sprays, and appear from September to January. The fruit is a short pod, 7 to 9 cm long, flat, with a distinctly rimmed margin. The pods mature from February to May.

This is one of the most beautiful of the indigenous trees; the showy yellow flowers are produced in profusion and make outstanding splashes of colour in the veld. Plants are now available from several nurseries.

The bark is used medicinally by the Africans. It is chewed to relieve colic, an infusion is used to relieve a variety of stomach disorders, and the steam from a hot decoction is used for sore eyes.

The wood is soft with a black heartwood. This has been used for carving, and it makes a good fuel.

This is the only species of *Peltophorum* which occurs in Rhodesia. Several Asiatic species are cultivated in Africa as ornamentals.

23 **PILIOSTIGMA THONNINGII** (Schumach.) Milne-Redh.

Plate 22

monkey bread
SH   *mutukutu*
N   *ihabahaba*

This species occurs from Senegal to the Sudan and southwards through Rhodesia to South West Africa, Botswana and the Transvaal.

It is common in the highveld woodlands and wooded grasslands. It is a medium sized, deciduous tree, usually 7 m to 9 m in height. The bark is rough and dark grey brown in colour.

The flowers are not conspicuous; male and female flowers are separate and appear from December to February. The fruit is a large, red brown pod, which does not split to release the seeds but simply falls to the ground and rots. The fruits mature from June to September.

The ash from the burnt wood is soapy and the green fruits are used by Africans as a substitute for soap. The bark contains a fibre which is used as string and is also made into rope.

A decoction of the bark is used in the treatment of coughs, and a mixture of the powdered roots and tobacco is said to be a stimulating drug.

The pods are much sought after by all types of game and also by stock. The ground pods produce a meal which is said to equal mealie meal in nutritional value and so are a very nourishing stock food. They tend to jam crushing machines if fresh, and so should be dried before they are ground. The wood makes a good fuel but other than this it has little value.

This is the only species of *Piliostigma* which occurs in Africa.

fuchsia tree, weeping boerboon
SH *mutondochuru*

This species reaches the northern limit of its range in Rhodesia at Mount Darwin. It also occurs in Moçambique and in South Africa from the eastern Cape, Natal and Swaziland, to the Transvaal.

In the Rhodesian highveld it almost always grows on termite mounds; it also occurs in the southern lowveld where it is often found along riverbanks.

This is a medium to large deciduous tree, usually about 10 m to 12 m in height, but it may be larger. The bark is brown grey in colour.

The flowers are produced in short sprays borne tightly against the old wood. The sepals are the most conspicuous part of the flower, varying from deep pink to dark blood red; the petals are absent or somewhat reduced (hence the specific name *brachypetala*, meaning 'short petals') and pink in colour. Nectar is produced in copious quantities, running from the flowers and even falling from the tree; this gives rise to its South African name, weeping boerboon—*boerboon* means 'farmer's bean' and comes from the fact that the seeds are edible. The nectar is much sought after by insects and birds, especially sunbirds. The flowers appear in September and October.

The fruit is a brown, flattened pod up to 10 cm long; the seeds are attractive, light brown in colour, with a bright yellow aril which envelops half the seed. The fruits mature from February to May.

A decoction of the bark is taken for heartburn, and is said to be an excellent remedy for a hang-over! It is apparently an emetic. The seed is edible, and the bark is used in tanning.

Another species of *Schotia*, *S. capitata*, occurs in the Gona-re-Zhou area. It is a much smaller tree, and is distinguished by its very dense heads of flowers (hence *capitata*), its well-formed petals, and the winged leaf rachis.

MIMOSOIDEAE (MIMOSA SUBFAMILY)

25 ACACIA KARROO Hayne   *Plate 25*

mimosa thorn, sweet thorn
SH *mubayamhondoro*
N *isinga*

This tree is found throughout the Republic of South Africa and as far north as Angola, Zambia, Malawi and Moçambique.

It occurs in a wide variety of habitats, but perhaps most frequently in wooded grassland and at vlei margins.

It is usually a medium sized, deciduous tree, up to 10 m in

height. The bark is smoothish, though sometimes fissured, and is dark brown to black in colour; the young branches are typically rusty coloured.

The flowers, in yellow, fluffy, sweetly scented balls, form loose heads near the ends of the branches and appear from December to March. The fruits, brown, flat, narrow pods, are sickle shaped, and mature from March to June.

Large quantities of a good quality gum exude from the trunk and branches. The gum is clear, amber coloured or red, has excellent adhesive properties and can be used in confectionery; for this purpose it used to be exported from South Africa as 'Cape Gum'. At one time the Forestry Department in Malawi supplied gum to the Government Printer for book-binding, and they also used it to make their own office glue.

The roots are used in African medicine; when they are burned and finely powdered they are rubbed into small cuts in the flesh to relieve lumbago; they are chewed as an aphrodisiac, and when soaked in water, the liquid is taken to treat gonorrhoea. A decoction is a Zulu emetic, and the crushed roots, mixed with food, are given to infants to relieve colic. The bark is used in tanning, and the inner bark makes a good rope widely used by farmers.

The presence of the tree is considered to indicate the sweetest and best grazing land. The leaves and fruits and even the old flowers form an excellent fodder. In the early days in the country its uses were almost unlimited: from fuel, fodder and fencing posts, to rope, shade tree, furniture and a useful general purpose timber, and even to protection from wild animals—the thorns are very effective indeed! Even today, farmers consider this one of the most valuable trees to have on a farm.

The paired thorns are stout, straight, white with a dark tip, and very large, 7 cm long being common, and in extreme cases even up to 17 cm long. These massive white thorns can present an impressive sight.

26 ACACIA POLYACANTHA Willd.
subsp. **CAMPYLACANTHA** (Hochst. ex A. Rich.)
Brenan   *Plate 26*
(*Acacia campylacantha* Hochst. ex A. Rich.)

hook thorn, white thorn
SH   *munanga*
N   *umohlo, umpumbu*

Typical *Acacia polyacantha*
is known only from India
and perhaps Ceylon. The
African subspecies *campylacantha* is widespread in
tropical Africa from Gam-
bia to Ethiopia and south to
the Transvaal.

It is most frequent in
wooded grassland and on
alluvial soils in river valleys. It is sometimes considered that these trees
indicate good, fertile soil
suitable for growing tobacco and cotton. It is a large,
handsome, deciduous tree,
up to 20 m in height. The
bark is pale in colour, inclined to be flaky, and may have strongly
hooked thorns on woody bosses; these are sometimes on the
trunk, but more particularly on the branches. The small branchlets are always thorny.

The flowers are in white or creamy spikes and appear from
October to March. The fruits are light brown, flat pods, only
8 to 13 cm long; they mature from April to October.

The wood burns well, but the thorns make it very difficult
to handle which is a drawback to its use as a fuel. The roots are
used by Africans to treat snake bite.

27 ACACIA SIEBERANA DC.
var. WOODII (Burtt Davy) Keay & Brenan   *Plate 27*

umbrella thorn, flat-topped thorn, paper-bark thorn
SH *muunga*
N *umlaladwayi*

Typical *Acacia sieberana* has
no hairs on the branchlets,
while var. *woodii* is distinguished by its hairy
branchlets. The species as a
whole is widespread in
tropical Africa from Senegal to Ethiopia and south to
the Transvaal and Natal.

It occurs in woodland
and wooded grassland and
is widespread.

This is a large deciduous
tree, widely branching, and
it is one of the most common of the 'flat-topped'
acacias; it can reach 17 m in
height, or it can be only
about 7 m in height with a comparatively immense spread. The
bark is light brown in colour.

The flowers form white, fluffy balls and appear from October
to December. The fruit is a creamy brown, woody pod up to 15
to 17 cm long, and matures from March onwards. The wood is
light, soft and of little value; it has a distinctive smell when
freshly cut.

In addition to the three species described in this book, there
are another thirty-six indigenous and two naturalised species of
Acacia in Rhodesia. Apart from the two naturalised Australian
species, the wattles, they are all armed with thorns. They range
in form from forest lianes (*Acacia pentagona*) to small shrubs
(*A. chariessa*); they are mostly trees, however, or at least sizeable
shrubs.

28 **ALBIZIA AMARA** (Roxb.) Boiv.
subsp. **SERICOCEPHALA** (Benth.) Brenan   *Plate 28*

SH *muora*
N *umbola*

The typical subspecies occurs in East Africa, India and Ceylon. The Rhodesian subspecies has a distribution from the Sudan and Ethiopia south to Botswana and the Transvaal. It is scattered in *Julbernardia-Brachystegia* woodland in the highveld and is often common on termite mounds. It is also found at lower altitudes.

It can be a large tree, reaching 14 m in height. The bark is grey to brown in colour and is rather rough and fissured. The young branches and leaves are finely golden velvety.

The leaflets are very fine and acacia-like. The flowers, typical of all the species of *Albizia*, are like powder puffs of silky stamens; the stamens are from 1 to 1,2 cm long. The flowers appear in September and October.

The fruit is a large, straight pod, 15 to 20 cm long, purplish when young, becoming brown to dark brown later. The pods mature from November to January. The fruits are used in African medicine, both as an emetic and as a cure for coughs and malaria. The roots contain saponin and are used as a substitute for soap for washing clothes. The wood rots quickly and is of little value.

There are two other Rhodesian species of *Albizia* with very small Acacia-like leaflets: *Albizia harveyi* occurs at lower altitudes and has slightly curved leaflets, and *Albizia brevifolia* is a small lowveld tree often dividing near the base into many ascending branches.

SH *muriranyenze*
N *umnonjwana*

Albizia antunesiana occurs from Zaire and Tanzania south to South West Africa, Botswana and Rhodesia. It is a common constituent of *Brachystegia-Julbernardia* woodland.

This is a medium sized, deciduous tree, rarely more than 10 m in height. The bark is rough, longitudinally fissured and grey in colour.

The flowers are the typical *Albizia* 'powder puffs', and are comparatively large, the stamens being up to 2,5 cm long; they appear from August to November.

The fruits are flat pods, purplish when young, becoming light brown when dry. The fruit splits to release the seeds and each half curls backwards, forming a ring. The fruits mature from April to September.

The bark and the roots are used in African medicine and tribal custom. The fresh roots are used as a dressing for wounds and sores, and are also used in a very generally known remedy for the common cold—here the roots are pounded and then boiled in water for ten minutes, when the steam from this is inhaled; this liquid is then allowed to cool and is drunk as a medicine. An infusion of the bark is applied to cuts to prevent them becoming septic, and the sap from the tree is used as eyedrops for inflamed and painful eyes.

It is the custom in parts of Malawi for the family of a deceased person to eat a specially prepared meal. For this a root, about 45 cm long, of *Albizia antunesiana* is collected, cut into small pieces, which are tied together and boiled up with beans in a pot.

Plate 29 ALBIZIA ANTUNESIANA, page 52

Plate 28 ALBIZIA AMARA, page 51

Plate 30   BOLUSANTHUS SPECIOSUS, page 55

Plate 31 ERYTHRINA ABYSSINICA, page 56

Plate 33 PERICOPSIS ANGOLENSIS, page 57

Plate 32 DICHROSTACHYS CINEREA, page 53

Plate 34 PTEROCARPUS ANGOLENSIS, page 59

Plate 35 SWARTZIA MADAGASCARIENSIS, page 61

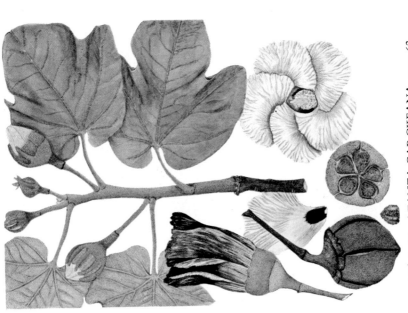

Plate 37 EKEBERGIA BENGUELENSIS, page 65

Plate 36 AZANZA GARCKEANA, page 63

Plate 39 FICUS BURKEI, page 67

Plate 38 TURRAEA NILOTICA, page 66

Plate 41 SYZYGIUM GUINEENSE, page 70

Plate 40 FICUS CAPENSIS, page 68

This is, in a way, the burial meal, with certain rites and cere-
monies attendant upon it; it is eaten immediately after the burial.

The wood is durable, resistant to termites and easy to work.
It resembles mukwa (*Pterocarpus angolensis*) in appearance and has
been used as a furniture wood, for joinery and also for plywood.
The African uses the wood to make drums and mortars, and also
as beaters for driving fish into his nets.

There are fifteen other species of *Albizia*, either indigenous or
naturalised, in Rhodesia; they are all fair sized trees.

30 DICHROSTACHYS CINEREA (L.) Wight & Arn.

(*D. glomerata* (Forsk.) Chiov.)   *Plate* 32

chinese lanterns
SH   *mupangara*
N   *ugagu*

This species is widespread
throughout tropical Africa
and occurs also in South
Africa. It extends through
tropical Asia to Indonesia
and Australia. It is ex-
tremely variable and has
been divided into several
subspecies and numerous
varieties. Three of the subspecies and six varieties are
recorded from Rhodesia,
but they are all extremely
similar to one another. It is
occasional in wooded grassland in a wide variety of
situations.

It is a small, scraggy tree
or shrub, about 3 to 4 m high, but it may be larger. The bark is
dark brownish grey in colour.

The flowers are clearly divided into two parts; half the flower
is formed by long, slender, pink, sterile staminodes, and the other

53

half is formed by the true flowers and is like a short, very compact, yellow catkin. The whole structure droops and hangs upside down on the tree, so the pink sterile part is above the yellow fertile section. The flowers appear from October to January. The pink section of the flowers varies in colour considerably in different areas, between trees in the same area, and even on the same tree, from almost white to mauve and bright pink. The generic name *Dichrostachys* comes from the Greek meaning 'two coloured flower spikes'.

The fruits are a cluster of twisted and contorted pods, and they mature between May and September. Cattle and game eat the fruits with great relish.

These trees often form secondary bush on impoverished soil, and so are often an indication of overgrazing. Under these conditions, *Dichrostachys cinerea* tends to form dense, impenetrable thickets.

Various parts of the tree are used to some extent in African medicine. The roots are chewed and then placed on snake bites and scorpion stings; the leaves are also used for this purpose and are said to produce a local anaesthesia. This reputed anaesthetic property is the reason for the application of leaves to relieve sore eyes, and to cure toothache. The Shona name *mupangara* means 'tassels for the chief's hat', and is a picturesque reference to the flowers.

The wood is extremely hard and durable. It has been used for poles and tool handles, but its use is somewhat limited by the small size of the tree. It is an excellent firewood, burning well but not too rapidly.

PAPILIONOIDEAE (PEA SUBFAMILY)

31 **BOLUSANTHUS SPECIOSUS** (Bolus) Harms *Plate* 30

tree wisteria
SH   *mupaka*
N   *impaca*

This genus contains only the one species which occurs in Rhodesia and all the countries bordering it, but it is not found further afield; its southern limit is reached in Natal. It is more common at lower altitudes and occurs in wooded grassland on a variety of soils.

This is a small, shapely, deciduous tree, 5 to 6 m in height. The bark is dark brown in colour, rough, and deeply fissured longitudinally.

The leaves are slender and hang gracefully so these, together with the beautiful flowers, make this tree most suitable as a garden plant. It is rather slow-growing and must be protected from frost, at least when young. It grows easily from seed and likes a well-drained soil.

The flowers are most attractive and hang on the tree in misty, mauve sprays in September and October. The fruits are small, thin, dirty-cream coloured pods and mature from March to May.

In the Transvaal Africans use the dried inner bark to relieve abdominal disorders. The wood is one of the best and hardest of indigenous timbers, and has a wide variety of uses.

erythrina, lucky-bean tree
SH *mutiti*
N *umgqogqogqo*

This species occurs from Zaire, Sudan and Ethiopia southwards to Moçambique and Rhodesia with a distinct subspecies occurring in Angola. It is a common tree of wooded grassland and grassland with scattered trees, and often grows on kopjes.

This is a medium sized tree, but heavy in its proportions, reaching 8 to 10 m in height, with the thickset trunk measuring up to 60 cm in diameter. The bark is light brown in colour.

The three very large, roundish leaflets often have prickles on their surfaces. The scarlet heads of flowers are spectacular, and these trees are always a feature of the landscape when in flower between July and November. The fruits are cylindrical pods, much constricted between the seeds, and are densely furry and light brown in colour. They mature between November and March.

The tree grows easily from a truncheon, planted in spring, and in three to four years will have reached a fair size. It should be protected from heavy frosts until it is well established.

The wood is soft and greyish white in colour, with a shot-silk effect. It is somewhat woolly to work with machines, but has been used for making stools, toys, drums and pestles. In years past it made splendid brake blocks for wagons as, being soft, it gripped tightly. The seeds are used in trinkets, bracelets, necklaces and are widely sold as curios. The seeds of *E. abyssinica* and

E. caffra (a South African species), and possibly the other species of *Erythrina*, too, contain a curare-like poison which, in quantity and if injected into the bloodstream, produces anaesthesia, paralysis and even death by respiratory failure. There is no danger in buying or selling these seeds, however, as it is very unlikely that, if swallowed, they would produce any effect at all.

The name *Erythrina* comes from the Greek word meaning 'red'.

The other Rhodesian species of *Erythrina* are also trees: *E. latissima* frequents granite kopjes on the highveld; *E. lysistemon* favours forest conditions in the Eastern Districts, but is also found in the south of the country and in the Matopos; and *E. livingstoniana* is a rare, spiny tree of the Sabi and Zambezi valleys.

33 **PERICOPSIS ANGOLENSIS** (Bak.) Van Meeuwen
(*Afrormosia angolensis* (Bak.) Harms)   *Plate* 33

afrormosia, muwanga
SH *muvanga*
N *umbanga*

Pericopsis angolensis reaches the northern limit of its range in Zaire and Tanzania, and does not occur further south than Angola, Rhodesia and Moçambique. It is locally common in open woodland and wooded grassland at medium to lower altitudes.

It is a beautiful, well-proportioned tree, usually from 10 m to 13 m in height. The bark is very characteristic, pale whitish grey or creamy brown in colour, smooth, with sparse, irregular flakes.

The flowers are usually whitish with a pink or mauve flush

and are carried in graceful sprays, but the colour can vary right through to a rich wine red. They appear from September to November. The fruits are flattened pods, up to 30 cm long, and are borne in distinctive, heavy clusters from June to October.

These trees are strongly fire-resistant, but are very sensitive to frost.

In Zambia a warm infusion of the bark and roots is used to bathe the eyes, and in Malawi an infusion of the leaves is used to relieve headaches—the leaves are pounded, then steeped in water in a pot, and the liquid used to bathe the face and head. It is said that the smell of the leaves alone is sometimes enough to cure a headache.

The wood is a fine, highly esteemed, general purpose timber; it is close-grained and virtually indestructable. It forms an excellent firewood, but is well known to farmers as one of the most valuable of timbers. Commercially it is known as *afrormosia* (for many years the tree was named *Afrormosia angolensis*), and is used for flooring blocks.

In Rhodesia the stands of this tree are not extensive enough, nor are the trees large enough, to be of great significance commercially, and all the timber is imported from Moçambique.

mukwa, kiaat
SH   *mubvamaropa*
N   *umvagazi*

Mukwa occurs in southern
Zaire and Tanzania in the
north and reaches its
southern limit in South
West Africa, Botswana, the
Transvaal and Swaziland.
It occurs in a number of
types of woodland and
wooded grassland in the
Rhodesian highveld.

It is usually a medium
sized, deciduous tree,
reaching 13 m in height.
These trees are seldom
large enough to yield timber on a commercial scale,
and most of the famous
furniture wood comes
from Moçambique, where mukwas reach heights of 20 m. The
bark is dark grey brown, and breaks up into squarish flakes.

The flowers, in attractive golden sprays, appear from August
to December. The fruit, technically a pod, is unusual in appearance: the single seed is covered with dense bristles, up to 1,5
cm long, and it is surrounded by a broad, papery, circular wing.
This prompted one person to say that it looked like a spiny fried
egg! These fruits develop from January to April.

The sap is red and sticky and oozes out when the tree is cut;
this blood-like sap is used by some African peoples as a cure for
nose bleeding—this is described under *Combretum zeyheri* (no. 9).
In addition to this, Africans have found uses for nearly all parts
of this tree.

The bark, when heated in water and then mixed with figs, is
used as a breast massage to induce lactation. A cold infusion of
the bark alone is used to ease nettle rash, and is also taken as a

cure for stomach disorders, headaches and ulcers in the mouth.

The bark, or the root, boiled with fresh meat is used as a preliminary accelerator in the cure for gonorrhoea, and a decoction of the root alone is used to treat malaria and blackwater fever. The cleaned roots are allowed to lie in water for six hours and then the liquid is used as an eyewash to treat corneal ulcers. As an additional, or follow-on, treatment, the flowers may be placed in boiling water, and the patient made to hold his face over this so that the steam fills his eyes. The flowers are also used to prepare an ointment for the treatment of ringworm; this is made by mixing together more or less equal parts of these crushed flowers, fowl manure and the fruits of a shrubby species of *Solanum*, burning all these and mixing the ashes with fat to form a paste. Very often the patch of ringworm is scrubbed vigorously with a dried maize cob before the ointment is smeared onto it.

These trees are very resistant to fire, but repeated, heavy burning produces a 'stag-headed' appearance, which occurs also if the tree is suffering under unfavourable conditions, such as shallow, stony soil, or too much water.

They grow easily from truncheons planted in October when the sap is rising. They make good garden subjects and truncheons are often planted around a chief's enclosure, so giving a fence of living trees.

This is one of the best known, most generally used and valuable of all woods found in Africa. It is highly esteemed as a first class furniture wood; it is easily worked, glues and screws well, and takes a fine polish. It shrinks very little when drying from the green condition and has been used with success in boat building because of its low shrinkage and high durability. The golden, or reddish brown, heartwood is used for high quality furniture, and Africans consider it one of the best woods for canoe construction. They also use it to make dishes, mortars and drums, and it is one of the few woods they use for canoe paddles and for their game and fish spears. The white sapwood is susceptible to borer attack, but the heartwood is very durable and is resistant to both borers and termites.

There are three other species of *Pterocarpus* growing in Rhodesia: *P. antunesii* occurs mainly in the Zambezi valley, and also sparingly in Gona-re-Zhou; *P. brenanii*, with the same distribution, has large, leaf-like stipules; and the widespread *P. rotundi-*

folius has been divided into two subspecies. None of these three species has the bristly fruits which are so characteristic of *P. angolensis*.

35 SWARTZIA MADAGASCARIENSIS Desv. *Plate 35*

snake bean
SH *mucherekese*
N *umketsheketshe*

This tree is widely distributed in tropical Africa extending from Gambia to Cameroun, Zaire and Tanzania and reaching its southern limit in South West Africa, Botswana, Rhodesia and Moçambique. It does not occur in Madagascar in spite of its specific name. It is common in *Julbernardia-Brachystegia* woodland and wooded grassland.

This is a small to medium sized, deciduous tree, reaching 10 m in height but usually much smaller. The bark is rough, longitudinally fissured and dark grey in colour. The flowers, unusual with their single, large, white petal, appear in October and November, but flowers may be found on the tree as late as January. The fruit, a long, cylindrical, dark red brown pod, may measure 30 cm in length and matures from April to September.

The pods have a far greater reputation as a poison than, apparently, they deserve. They are widely used as a fish poison, in this context with some justification as the powdered pods succeeded in killing goldfish in a test trial, though a fairly high concentration was necessary. They are also used by bushmen in the preparation of their arrow poison, but this poison, injected subcutaneously into a cat, produced little effect. The powdered pods have also been used with murderous intent, the powder being slipped into the beer of an unwanted person. Wild game and cattle eat the pods with impunity, however, though in cattle this tends to taint the milk. So it seems that in spite of its widespread acceptance as a poison there is little substance to this belief, but as a fish poison it is effective, although of low toxicity. It is also used as an insecticide and as an insect repellant, and often, in order to keep grain free of termites and weevils, grain storage bins are lined with powder made by pulverising the pods.

In Zambia a decoction of the pods is used in the treatment of leprosy.

The wood is even and close-grained; it is usually red brown in colour and can develop a purplish black heartwood which is very decorative. It is extremely durable and termite-resistant, and is used for carving, handicraft, cabinet work and inlay. Visitors to the Victoria Falls will be familiar with the small curios, ashtrays and jars which the Africans make from this wood and sell to tourists; it is considered second only to mpingo (*Dalbergia melanoxylon*) for making candlesticks, cigarette boxes and other small ornaments.

36 AZANZA GARCKEANA (F. Hoffm.) Exell & Hillcoat
(*Thespesia garckeana* F. Hoffm.)   Plate 36

snot apple, tree hibiscus, quarters
SH   *mutohwe*
N   *uxhakhuxhaku*

This tree occurs in east tropical Africa as far north as the Sudan Republic and it is widespread in south tropical Africa extending into South Africa.

It occurs in woodland, wooded grassland and is often found growing on termite mounds. It is not confined to the highveld, being found from sea level to 2 000 m.

It is a small to medium sized, deciduous tree, usually 5 m to 7 m in height, but quite thickset; it may reach 10 m in height, however, in some localities. The bark is rough and brown in colour.

The large, yellow, showy flowers are borne singly in the axils of the leaves, and appear from January to March. The colour of the petals changes from clear yellow to a reddish orange as they start to fade.

The fruits are almost spherical, 2,5 to 4 cm long, and they are clearly divided into four to five sections; this has given the tree the common name, quarters. The fruits mature from May to October. They are densely furry and the outer covering is hard and woody. Nevertheless, the fruits are edible, and if the inner part is chewed with perseverance a sweet, glutinous slime is produced. The Ndebele name *uxhakhuxhaku* represents the noise one makes when chewing the fruit.

The wood has little value, but has been used for making tool handles.

Only this one species of *Azanza* occurs in Africa.

MELIACEAE (MAHOGANY FAMILY)

37 **EKEBERGIA BENGUELENSIS** Welw. ex DC.
(*E. arborea* Bak. f.)   *Plate* 37

SH   *muvhuranyimo*

This tree occurs from Zaire and Tanzania southwards to Angola, Zambia, Rhodesia and Moçambique. It occurs in woodland and wooded grassland at medium altitudes.

The size of this deciduous tree is variable, from 3 m to 13 m; the latter is probably a maximum, and the trees most commonly seen are considerably smaller. The bark is dark grey in colour and it is inclined to be flaky.

The flowers are small, white or slightly flushed with pink, and are carried in short sprays about 6 to 8 cm long which appear in September and October. The fruit is an edible berry about the size of a cherry. Birds are very fond of these when they mature in November and December.

Certain parts of this tree are used by African girls in the fertility rites which accompany marriage.

One other species of *Ekebergia* is found in Rhodesia. This is *E. capensis*, a forest species; it can be distinguished by its second year branchlets which are more slender, usually less than 6 mm in diameter, and are liberally dotted with large, white lenticels.

SH   *chipindura*
N   *isidlamvundala*

This species is widespread
in east and south tropical
Africa reaching its northern
limit in the Sudan Repub-
lic and its southern limit in
the Transvaal.

It most commonly oc-
curs as a tree of wooded
grassland, but is also found
on termite mounds and as
a riverine species in the
south-eastern lowveld. It is
a small, deciduous tree, 3 m
to 6 m in height. The bark
is rough and grey in colour.

The large, simple leaves
are unusual for this family
in which compound leaves
are generally found. The flowers are whitish green and inconspicuous, but they are produced in profusion from June to
September and are much sought after by hordes of insects. The
fruits, maturing in October and November, are attractive and
lend themselves for use in floral arrangements.

In general appearance it is easy to confuse this small tree with
Vangueriopsis lanciflora (no. 49); however, the bark of *Turraea* is
rough and grey, while that of *Vangueriopsis* is smooth and light
brown, and the young branches of *Vangueriopsis* are conspicuously
rusty coloured and powdery, while those of *Turraea* are not. The
fruits are very different.

Africans use the roots to relieve liver and stomach pains; the
roots are crushed, warmed with a little water and added to porridge, which is eaten three times a day until the pain is relieved.

Four other species of *Turraea* occur in Rhodesia, but *T. nilotica*
is by far the most common. *T. zambesica* grows only in the
Zambezi valley, *T. fischeri* subsp. *eylesii* has been recorded only

from the Matopos, and *T. floribunda* is a fairly widespread tree of forest edges. The fourth species, *T. obtusifolia*, is a shrub and is found growing on granite kopjes.

MORACEAE (FIG FAMILY)

39　**FICUS BURKEI** (Miq.) Miq.
　　(*F. rhodesiaca* Warb. ex Mildbr. & Burret)　　　　*Plate 39*

wild fig
SH　*mutsamvi*
N　*intenjane*

This species is widespread in Africa from Zaire and Tanzania southwards, through Rhodesia and into South Africa. At one time, specimens with hairy leaves were separated as *F. rhodesiaca*, but the surface covering on the leaves is so variable that this is not considered to be a valid distinction, and the species *F. rhodesiaca* has been dropped.

It is found in a wide variety of habitats, from various types of woodland to rocky kopjes and termite mounds.

These large, spreading trees can reach 10 m in height. The bark is smooth and light grey in colour.

This is one of the figs which produces the 'fruits' towards the tips of the branches among the leaves. (Compare this with the next species, *F. capensis*, no. 40.) The figs are small, furry and, though edible, have little flavour and are not very palatable; they are eagerly sought after by birds, however, especially green pigeons, grey loeries and glossy starlings.

40 FICUS CAPENSIS Thunb. *Plate 40*

cape fig
SH *mukuyu*
N *umkhiwa*

The cape fig is widespread in tropical and South Africa from Senegal to the Cape Province. This tree is common in a variety of habitats at most altitudes and may occur in riverine vegetation, on granite kopjes or in wooded grassland.

It is a large, spreading tree, reaching 12 m in height and may be much larger in some areas. The bark is smooth and grey in colour, and great bunches of figs are produced on the main stem and branches.

It is an interesting botanical detail that the figs are not, in fact, fruits; they are formed by the fleshy receptacle growing upwards and over to form a hollow sphere, and inside this are many tiny flowers. Through a small opening at the end of the growing fig,

Plate 43 XIMENIA CAFFRA, page 73

Plate 42 OCHNA PULCHRA, page 71

Plate 44   SECURIDACA LONGEPEDUNCULATA, page 75

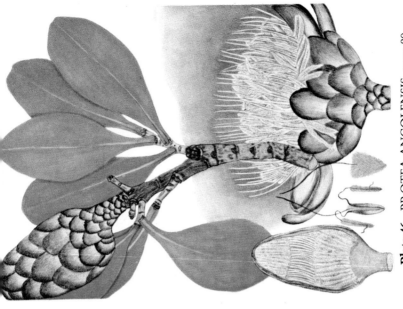

Plate 46 PROTEA ANGOLENSIS, page 80

Plate 45 FAUREA SALIGNA, page 78

Plate 47   GARDENIA SPATULIFOLIA, page 83

Plate 49 VANGUERIOPSIS LANCIFLORA, page 85

Plate 48 ZIZIPHUS MUCRONATA, page 81

Plate 51 DOMBEYA ROTUNDIFOLIA, page 88

Plate 50 SALIX SUBSERRATA, page 86

Plate 52 STERCULIA QUINQUELOBA, page 90
(Head of leaves and flowers greatly reduced in size)

Plate 54 VITEX PAYOS, page 92

Plate 53 STRYCHNOS COCCULOIDES, page 91

minute wasps enter to lay their eggs, and at the same time pollinate the female flowers by bringing in pollen from a mature fig. As well as carrying pollen to the fig, the wasps also carry nematodes, or eelworms, of many different species. The nematodes reproduce within the fig and are sometimes found in enormous numbers. It is intriguing to ponder upon how the association developed between the figs, wasps and nematodes. The true fruits are minute, single-seeded nuts, and it is the whole collection of these which gives an old fig its slightly gritty texture when eaten.

These figs are not particularly pleasant to eat; the flavour is disappointing and they are normally full of insects. They can be used to make jam, but the flavour is insipid unless some other fruit, such as apple, is added. They do make good pig and cattle feed, however.

The Zulus drink a decoction of the root and bark for lung ailments, and they give an infusion of the root, bark and leaves to cows to increase the milk supply; this is possibly a superstition linked with the milky latex produced by the tree.

There are some twenty other species of fig which occur in Rhodesia, ranging from huge forest stranglers like *F. kirkii* in Chirinda Forest at Mount Selinda to the streamside species *F. verruculosa* which can fruit as a dwarf shrub or form a sizeable tree, depending on soil conditions. The species most likely to be confused with *F. capensis* is *F. sycomorus* which also has figs in large bunches on the main trunk. It can be readily distinguished by its rough leaves, the leaves of *F. capensis* being smooth on the upper surface. The pale, yellowish trunk of *F. sycomorus* is also distinctive.

MYRTACEAE (EUCALYPTUS AND GUAVA FAMILY)

41 SYZYGIUM GUINEENSE (Willd.) DC. *Plate 41*

waterberry
SH *mukute*
N *imiswi*

This species as a whole has a wide distribution in tropical Africa and also extends into South Africa. There are two subspecies which occur in Rhodesia, subsp. *barotsense* and subsp. *macrocarpum*; subsp. *macrocarpum* is the more widespread of these and it is the one more likely to be encountered in the open woodlands of the central watershed.

It is a medium sized, well-shaped, deciduous tree reaching a height of about 12 m. The bark is roughish and grey in colour.

The flowers, appearing from June to October, are typical of the family, with a head of stamens resembling *Eucalyptus* flowers. The fruits, dark purple berries, are edible and quite pleasant when fully ripe, otherwise they are very sour. They can be used to make a good quality vinegar. The fruits mature from October to January.

In some areas an infusion of the roots is used medicinally to bathe a patient if an illness has become serious. For example, if the patient should become delirious he would be bathed with this infusion which is said to check the delirium.

The wood is pale red in colour. It is hard, strong and easy to work, and is said to be durable. It has been used to make dug-out canoes.

Five other indigenous species of *Syzygium* occur in Rhodesia:
S. huillense is a dwarf species of vleis; *S. gerrardii* is the dominant
species in some of the forests of the Eastern Districts; *S. cordatum*
is a common stream bank species which hybridises freely with
S. guineense; *S. masukuense* is a high altitude forest species and *S.
owariense* is a low altitude forest species. Two further species,
S. jambos and *S. cuminii*, have become locally naturalised.

OCHNACEAE (OCHNA FAMILY)

42 **OCHNA PULCHRA** Hook.
      subsp. **PULCHRA**   *Plate 42*

peeling-bark ochna
SH *muminu*
N *umnyelenyele*

This species occurs from
Zaire to South West Afri-
ca, Botswana, the Trans-
vaal, Rhodesia and Mo-
çambique. It has not yet
been recorded from Ma-
lawi.

The typical subspecies is
replaced in Angola, Zaire
and north-western Zambia
by subsp. *hoffmani-ottonis*.

In Rhodesia it is usually
a small, deciduous tree, 4 m
to 6 m tall. The outer, grey
bark peels off the stem and
older branches in thin,
woody flakes which hang
on the stem, revealing the
beautiful, delicately coloured, pearly, smooth underbark; this is
very characteristic.

The creamy yellow petals fall soon, only hours after the flower
opens. The sepals are persistent, light green at first, becoming

shell pink as the fruits develop; sometimes this colour may deepen to red. These colourful sepals are frequently mistaken for the petals of the flower. The true flowers appear fleetingly in September and October, and later the attractive sepals take on their colour as the fruits develop from November to March.

The fruits are about the size of a pea, slightly kidney shaped, and one to three develop in each 'flower'. The fruits are rich in oil which has been used to make a fair quality soap.

A small piece of the root is often carried as a talisman; a man seeking work may slip a root into his pocket, and even hunters carry a piece as a lucky charm.

Eighteen other species of *Ochna* occur naturally in Rhodesia, ranging from tall forest trees like *O. holstii* to dwarf species like *O. leptoclada*. The most common species of the Rhodesian highveld woodland is *O. schweinfurthiana*; *O. pulchra* may be distinguished from this by its almost entire leaves and the peeling bark.

OLACACEAE

43 **XIMENIA CAFFRA** Sond.

Plate 43

sour plum
SH   *mutengeni, mutsvanzwa*
N   *umthunduluka*

This species occurs from Zaire, Uganda and Kenya southwards to the Cape Province in South Africa. It is common in woodland and wooded grassland in both the highveld and the lowveld; it may occur on rocky slopes and quite often grows on termite mounds.

It is a small, evergreen tree, 3 m to 5 m in height, often straggling and sometimes definitely a shrub. The branches are always spiny, the spines being simple and straight, formed from modified, abortive branchlets. The bark is rough on larger specimens, and dark grey in colour.

The small, insignificant, whitish flowers have bearded petals, and arise in tight clusters in the axils of the young leaves. The flowers appear from August to October. The fruits, red, fleshy and containing a single hard stone, mature in November and December; they are edible but very sour.

The leaves are densely rusty hairy when young. In mature leaves the upper surface may lose much of this hairiness, but the lower surface remains conspicuously furry.

There is a sixty-five per cent yield of oil from the kernels of the fruits. It is a good, pale, viscous, non-drying oil which has been used in curing animal hides.

The leaves and roots are used in African medicine. A cold

infusion of the leaves is used for inflamed eyes. An infusion of the roots has a purgative effect and is used in the treatment of bilharzia, hookworm and syphilis. In the western areas of Zambia, a decoction of the roots is used to cure a strange malady called *liyaya*, the symptoms of which appear to be a swollen abdomen, loss of appetite, nausea, and weakness in the arms. To diagnose the disease the doctor requires three drums, and the drummers start beating these at dawn; all through the day the rhythm is beaten out, and the patient is made to sit on the ground, legs outstretched. If this test is positive then his legs start moving in time to the drumbeats and the doctor begins treatment without delay. With the beating drums as a background, the roots of *X. caffra* are boiled in water and a large spoonful is administered five times during the day. In addition a hot fomentation is made from the leaves of a tree, *Erythrophleum africanum*, and is applied to the distended stomach. At one time the doctor charged $1 for this treatment, which seems very modest as this included the provision of the drums.

There is only one other species of *Ximenia*, *X. americana*, and this also occurs in Rhodesia. It can be distinguished from *X. caffra* by the flowers which are in short sprays, and also by the leaves which are usually without hairs.

44 SECURIDACA LONGEPEDUNCULATA Fresen.

Plate 44

violet tree
SH *mufufu*
N *umfumfu*

This species is widespread in tropical Africa from West Africa and Ethiopia southwards to South West Africa, Botswana, the Transvaal, Rhodesia and Moçambique.

The violet tree occurs as a scattered tree in woodland and wooded grassland at most altitudes. It is a deciduous tree, usually only 3 m to 4 m in height, but it can reach 9 m if growing under very favourable conditions. The bark is smoothish and light grey in colour.

The flowers are beautiful, in short sprays, and very sweetly scented; they appear with the young leaves in August and September, although the flowering season may continue on into October and November.

The fruits, each with a single, brittle wing, up to 5 cm long, are purplish green when young, becoming a pale straw colour when dry; they mature from April to August.

There is no doubt that the roots of this tree contain poisonous properties, and their use represents the accepted means of suicide for the women of the Lovale tribes in Zambia. The roots, crushed or powdered, are used as an intra-vaginal poison and there have been many authenticated cases reported and recorded over the years by medical officers stationed in this area. Dr W.

Gilges has quoted a number of case histories in his occasional paper, 'Some African Poison Plants and Medicines of Northern Rhodesia'. The case of the old woman who was accused of witch-craft and, rather than face ostracism by the village, killed herself by this method, is one. All the cases were tragic and pathetic stories of lonely women driven to the point of absolute despair, often by trivial little problems, such as the woman who had an argument with her husband over the sum of two cents. In all the cases he examined, Dr Gilges found the same pattern of poisoning symptoms: rapid pulse rate, repeated vomiting and extreme weakness, with death following sometimes within thirty-six hours. Post-mortem examinations showed multiple submucous haemorrhages in the respiratory system, the stomach, intestines, bladder and uterus, with a complete breakdown of the vaginal mucosa.

It seems that these poisonous properties are well known to these people, but they are emphatic that they are effective only if introduced into the vagina or rectum. Nevertheless, an infusion of the roots is used by Africans elsewhere to destroy marauding dogs, and in West Africa a compound of the juice is sometimes used as an arrow poison.

Root scrapings contain much methyl salicylate and so have the strong, characteristic smell of oil of wintergreen; this is supposed to drive snakes away.

No doubt as a result of the known poisonous properties of the roots, they are used sometimes for associated problems. In 1943, eight deaths from *Securidaca* poisoning were reported by the medical officer in the Balovale area of Zambia, and two of these were young girls who had the roots administered by an African doctor in an attempt to procure abortions. It is widely used as an abortifacient in Rhodesia, often with very harmful effects. The roots are used also as a contraceptive, and the whole matter is surrounded by mysticism and myth: scrapings of the inner roots are added to gunpowder and mixed with water, then the woman must stand at the cross roads, facing west, and drink this mixture through an old, used and long-discarded axe handle. Almost certainly its reputation is more effective than the treatment itself!

The leaves, pounded with water and salt, are taken to relieve coughs, and the roots themselves are used for more orthodox treatments—an infusion is used as a mouthwash in cases of toothache, and is applied to cuts in the legs to cure inflammatory conditions. A powder produced from the burnt roots is rubbed into small cuts made on the temples and forehead to relieve headaches.

A good fibre is obtained from the bark, and this is used to make fishing nets and as thread to sew bark cloth. On the Zambezi the Africans use the bark as soap, and the leaves to treat snake bite.

This beautiful tree is difficult to cultivate. The seeds are difficult to germinate, and young plants do not transplant well, but the tree would make a beautiful addition to any garden and it would be well worthwhile to persevere and try to get at least one plant established.

This is the only species of *Securidaca* which occurs in Rhodesia. Another species, with equally showy flowers, occurs as a climbing shrub or liane in the evergreen forests of north-western Zambia.

PROTEACEAE (PROTEA FAMILY)

45 **FAUREA SALIGNA** Harv. *Plate 45*

faurea, boekenhout
SH *mutsatsati*
N *umdwadwa*

This species extends as far north as Nigeria, Uganda and Kenya, and reaches the Transvaal and Natal in the south. It is a common tree of the *Julbernardia-Brachystegia* woodlands of the central watershed. A very similar tree that grows along stream banks with wider and sparingly hairy leaves may be separable as a subspecies.

This is a tall, deciduous tree, usually up to 12 m high, always graceful in shape and occasionally reaching 18 m in height. The bark is rough, longitudinally furrowed, and dark, brownish grey in colour.

The flowers form a dense spike, up to 10 or 14 cm long, and appear from August to November. The fruits mature from October to January.

This tree is quite easy to recognise as it looks rather like a small-leaved *Eucalyptus* (gum tree).

The roots feature in African medicine. In the Mtoko area the roots are shredded, soaked in water for a day, and two large spoonfuls of this mixture are given daily in the treatment of gonorrhoea. In Zambia the roots are used in the treatment of dysentery. Some of the roots are made into a porridge with either beans or groundnuts, and this is given to the patient to eat; then pieces of the root are soaked in cold water for about ten minutes and half a cup is given twice a day for three days. The same liquid is administered as an enema, using a small calabash as a syringe.

The wood is excellent; light cream to red in colour with a beautiful reticulated grain, it is strong, durable, and borer-proof. It is easy to work and polishes well. There is some resemblance to the European beech, which gave rise to the South African common name, *boekenhout*. It is valuable as a furniture wood and also for general joinery. Trunks have been used as fencing posts, and they last well; the original telephone poles between the old South African Republic (now the Transvaal) and Natal are said to have been trunks of *Faurea saligna*. It is also an excellent firewood.

The wood, soaked in water, produces a red dye, and the bark has been used in tanning.

The name *Faurea* was given to the genus by Harvey in the nineteenth century as a tribute to a young soldier, Mr W. C. Faure, 'a young man of much promise, and a most ardent botanist'. When trying to rejoin his regiment in India, Faure was ambushed in difficult country and was shot and killed by some unknown person. The specific name *saligna* means 'willow-like' and refers to the drooping leaves.

Two other species of *Faurea* occur in Rhodesia: *F. forficuliflora* is a forest species from the Eastern Districts and has showy red to crimson red flowers; *F. speciosa* is a woodland species with broad, hairy leaves, and is less widespread than *F. saligna*, being absent from the west and south of the country.

46 **PROTEA ANGOLENSIS** Welw.
var. **DIVARICATA** (Engl. & Gilg) Beard   Plate 46

protea, sugar bush
SH *mubonda*
N *isiqalaba*

This species occurs from
Zaire and Tanzania south
to Angola, Zambia and
Rhodesia. The typical
variety is a dwarf species
not more than 50 cm in
height and var. *divaricata* is
a deciduous shrub or tree
which occurs in woodland
and wooded grassland, and
reaches a height of about
3 m to 4 m. The roughish
bark is grey in colour.

The flowers appear from
April to July, and the fruits
mature from June to
August.

In South Africa the common name *suikerbos*, or sugar bush, is
applied generally to all species of *Protea*, and it seems to have
come from the fact that the flowers produce copious nectar which
is rich in sugar; this is more noticeable in some species than in
others. The nectar is sought after by insects, particularly ants.

The wood forms a good charcoal. Africans make an infusion
by placing the bark and roots in a small pot with some water,
and they use this to bathe newly born babies to ensure that they
grow into strong and healthy children.

There are eight other species of *Protea* occurring naturally in
Rhodesia. Five are endemic species of the Chimanimani and
Inyanga mountains. Of the remaining three, *P. gaguedi* is widespread, but with narrower leaves than *P. angolensis*; *P. welwitschii*
is also common but with hairy leaves; *P. petiolaris*, in which the
leaves are narrowed at the base into a pseudo-petiole, is a species
of *Brachystegia* woodland at higher altitudes.

RHAMNACEAE (BUFFALO THORN FAMILY)

47 ZIZIPHUS MUCRONATA Willd. subsp. RHODESICA R. B. Drummond

Plate 48

buffalo thorn
SH *muchecheni*
N *umphafa*

The typical subspecies, subsp. *mucronata*, has a wide distribution from Senegal to Ethiopia and Arabia and extending as far south as the Cape Province in South Africa. The second subspecies, subsp. *rhodesica*, is distinguished by the coarse, brownish, woolly hairs on the undersurface of the leaves. It is widespread in Rhodesia and Zambia, and extends marginally into the surrounding countries, Zaire, Tanzania, Malawi, Moçambique and Botswana.

It occurs mainly in *Julbernardia-Brachystegia* woodland and wooded grassland, and often grows on termite mounds. At lower altitudes it is replaced by subsp. *mucronata*, which has very few hairs on its leaves.

It is a medium sized, deciduous, spreading tree up to 10 m in height. The bark is roughish and brown to grey in colour. The flowers are small and inconspicuous, appearing in January and February; there is often a second flowering season in August and September. The round, red brown, glossy fruits appear in May and June, and again in November and December. The leaves are particularly susceptible to insect attack and this often gives the tree a ragged appearance.

The roots, bark and leaves are quite widely used in African

medicine. The leaves are chewed as an aphrodisiac; an infusion of the roots is used to treat dysentery; and a decoction of the roots is used to prevent the development of elephantiasis, and is also used as an abortifacient. A powder made by drying and pounding the roots is rubbed into small cuts made on the chest in cases of pneumonia.

Extracts of the bark and leaves have been found to contain tannin.

The berries are edible, although not particularly pleasant tasting, and are eaten chiefly by birds. In southern Malawi, however, these berries are used to make an extremely potent alcoholic drink called *kachaso*. The berries are gathered from the ground after they have fallen from the tree and so are fully ripe and already slightly fermenting. These fruits are put into a large pot, an old gun barrel is fixed into the top of the pot, all the openings are carefully sealed and the pot is strongly heated. The vapour from the boiling fruits travels down the gun barrel which is kept cool by water being constantly poured over it. As the vapour condenses a clear, colourless liquid drips from the muzzle of the barrel and is carefully collected in containers.

The wood is pinkish white or yellow streaked with red and, although it is tough and elastic, it warps badly and is not durable, so it has only limited use.

These trees are usually very thorny, but this is variable, some specimens having few thorns or no thorns at all. The common name, buffalo thorn, dates back to the very early days in South Africa, when farmers used the branches for building their kraals to protect their cattle and horses, and themselves, from the wild animals, possibly including buffalo.

The leaves and the fruits are browsed by game and can be a useful source of fodder for stock animals in times of drought.

The generic name *Ziziphus* comes from *zizouf*, the Arabic name for *Z. lotus*; the specific name *mucronata* means 'a fine, sharp point' and possibly refers to the thorns.

Four other species of *Ziziphus* occur in Rhodesia: *Z. pubescens* is devoid of thorns and is a rare species found in the dry, low-lying areas of the country; *Z. mauritiana*, with a pleasantly edible fruit, is widely naturalised in the north of Rhodesia close to the border with the Tete province of Moçambique—it is grown for its fruits; *Z. zeyherana* is a dwarf shrublet of the highveld; and

Z. abyssinica, occurring along the Zambezi escarpment, is very similar to *Z. mucronata* subsp. *rhodesica*, but can be distinguished by the grey, uniformly furry underside of the leaves, and by the absence of hairs on the upper surface.

RUBIACEAE (COFFEE FAMILY)

48 GARDENIA SPATULIFOLIA Stapf & Hutch. *Plate 47*

gardenia
SH *mutara*
N *umvalasangwani*

This species is widely distributed in tropical Africa and reaches its southern limit in South West Africa, Botswana, Swaziland, the Transvaal and Natal.

It is common in woodland and wooded grassland at both medium and low altitudes, often occurring on termite mounds particularly at medium altitudes.

It is a shrub, or a small, deciduous tree rarely reaching 7 m in height, often straggling and short-boled, with intricately tortuous branches. There are, in fact, no spines present, but the dwarf, rigid, lateral branches are so tough as to be almost spinescent.

The flowers are large, beautiful, waxy white when young, turning yellow with age. They are deliciously scented and appear from September to November.

The fruits are quite large, almost spherical, hard and fibrous, with a rough, encrusted covering. They mature from December to April.

The roots are used in African medicine, and the wood, white, fine-grained, hard and heavy, is used by Africans for carving ornaments. The small size of the pieces of wood prevents their use for very much else.

These plants are easily propagated from cuttings or from seed. They are fairly fast-growing and are a worthy addition to any garden, given a warm situation and a well-drained soil. Each flower is short-lived, but one follows the other in succession, so the flowering season is reasonably extended.

The genus *Gardenia* was named after Alexander Garden, a physician in South Carolina, and the specific name means 'with leaves shaped like a spatula'.

Four other species of *Gardenia* occur naturally in Rhodesia, all of them with the characteristic, white, sweetly scented flowers. *G. jovis-tonantis* differs in leaf shape and hairiness and in the fruit shape and colour, but is otherwise very similar to *G. spatulifolia* in appearance and ecology; *G. imperialis* and *G. posoquerioides* are forest species; and *G. resiniflua* is a species with small flowers common in dry situations at low altitudes.

49 VANGUERIOPSIS LANCIFLORA (Hiern) Robyns

Plate 49

false medlar
SH   *mutufu*
N   *amadumbutshene, umviyo*

This tree occurs from Zaire and Tanzania southwards to South West Africa, Botswana and Rhodesia. It is common in the *Brachystegia-Julbernardia* woodlands and wooded grasslands of the central watershed, but is apparently absent from the south and east of the country.

It is a small, semi-deciduous tree, rarely more than 4 m in height. The bark is smooth, light brown in colour, and often with a powdery covering; the young branches are thick, brittle, and a conspicuous, reddish brown colour.

The flowers are insignificant and the narrow, white petals curve backwards. They appear from August to October. The fruits are markedly asymmetrical; they are green when young, turning yellowish when ripe, and mature in November and December. They are edible but have a disappointing, insipid taste.

The powdery bark is used by African doctors to treat mumps. The powder is scraped off the branches, mixed with a grain meal and worked to a paste with a little water. The patient is isolated, and this paste is rubbed onto the swellings round the face and neck. The doctors expect rapid relief and consider it unlikely that the treatment would have to last longer than one day.

Truncheons from this tree take root easily and grow rapidly.

Only one species of *Vangueriopsis* occurs in Rhodesia: *Vangueria infausta* has very similar foliage, but the flowers and fruits are very much smaller and the branches are not reddish brown.

SALICACEAE (WILLOW FAMILY)

50 **SALIX SUBSERRATA** Willd.

Plate 50

willow
SH *mutepe*
N *umnyezane*

This is a widespread species in tropical Africa and reaches Libya, Egypt, Israel and Syria in the north and South West Africa, Botswana, Rhodesia and the Transvaal in the south.

It is a common shrub or small tree of river and stream banks and islands, usually in places that are likely to become inundated at least for a brief period during the year. Seldom exceeding 7 m in height, it is often flattened and distorted by the force of the surging waters when the rivers are in flood. The tree is deciduous, but unexpectedly drops its leaves in summer, possibly as a response to the summer flooding of the rivers. The bark is deeply longitudinally fissured and dark brown in colour.

The flowers are inconspicuous, forming short spikes; the male and female flowers are separate, and appear, with two flowering seasons, in March and April and again in August and September. The fruits are very small, not much larger than the flowers they replace, and split to release the seeds, each one provided with a tuft of silvery hairs. The fruits mature in June and July and again in April.

If the young branches are carefully tapped, the bark can be slipped off the wood and children can use this to make very good whistles.

In years now past, a group of these trees was taken as an indication of harder ground: a place where the river could be forded safely, either on horseback or with wagons.

The Africans use the roots as a cure for headaches and fevers.

This is the only species of *Salix* which occurs naturally in Rhodesia. The weeping willow, *Salix babylonica*, is introduced and has been widely planted along streams and by dams.

STERCULIACEAE

51 **DOMBEYA ROTUNDIFOLIA** (Hochst.) Planch.

Plate 51

wild pear
SH *mutongotowa*
N *umwane*

This species occurs from
Zaire, Uganda and Kenya
southwards to South West
Africa, Botswana, Rho-
desia, the Transvaal and
Natal. It is widespread in
woodland and wooded
grassland. In some areas it
shows a preference for termite mounds.

It is a shapely, deciduous
tree, capable of reaching
heights of 7 m to 8 m, but
usually attaining considerably less. The bark is deeply
longitudinally furrowed
and is dark brown in
colour.

The flowers are very decorative, pure white and sweet smelling;
the petals are persistent, slowly becoming yellowish brown and
papery. The flowers appear from July to October, and occasionally may be tinged pale pink. They are visited by bees. The
fruit is a small capsule and matures from October to December.

This is one of the earliest of the spring-flowering trees, and
while the whole countryside is still brown and dry after winter,
the wild pear makes conspicuous patches of snowy white. This
is a very good tree to introduce into the garden, and in fact grows
quite quickly under good garden conditions, although it is rather
slow in the wild. It can be raised easily from seed and will tolerate
several degrees of frost. The seed should be planted in September.

The trees withstand fire well, and the wood makes good fuel.
The wood itself is heavy, strong, tough and a bluish grey in

colour. Its small size limits its use, but it has the properties of an excellent general purpose timber. Africans use the wood to make bows and tool handles.

The Zulus use an infusion of the bark or wood to treat intestinal ulcers, and the Shangaan women drink a decoction of the bark to hasten the onset of labour.

Two other species of *Dombeya* occur naturally in Rhodesia: the pink-flowered *D. burgessiae* occurs most frequently as a forest-edge shrub or small tree; and *D. kirkii* is a smaller, white-flowered species common in riverine vegetation at lower altitudes.

52 **STERCULIA QUINQUELOBA** (Garcke) K. Schum.

Plate 52

SH *mungoza*
N *umkukubuyu*

This species occurs from Zaire and Tanzania south to South West Africa, Zambia, Rhodesia and Moçambique.

A striking tree, it is often a feature of rocky hills and slopes. It is a large, deciduous tree, 10 m to 12 m in height, with thickset trunk and branches. The bark is cream to pinkish brown and, except for odd flakes, is smooth and rather shiny.

The very large leaves, conspicuously five-lobed, are crowded at the ends of the branches, and turn beautiful yellows and golds in autumn just before they fall. The heads of yellowish flowers are not conspicuous, and are produced from January to April.

The fruits are very striking: they consist of five separate carpels, each splitting along the line of attachment of the seeds; they are golden velvety on the outside, smooth inside, with a circle of unpleasant, irritating bristles round the edge of the opening, among the seeds. The fruits mature from May to September.

The wood is reddish brown and has been used as a mining timber in general construction work, and for furniture.

The trees exude a good quality gum, but they do not tap well and the flow of gum tends to be seasonal, so it cannot be exploited as a commercial proposition.

There are three other indigenous species of *Sterculia* in Rhodesia: *S. africana* is widespread at lower altitudes; *S. appendiculata*, a tall tree with a straight, unbranched bole, is found very sparingly in the lower Mazoe valley; and *S. rogersii* is a small tree, branching low down, common in the Sabi valley and southern lowveld.

STRYCHNACEAE (MONKEY-ORANGE FAMILY)

53 **STRYCHNOS COCCULOIDES** Bak. *Plate 53*

monkey-orange
SH   *mutamba-muzhinyu*
N   *umkhemethswane*

This species occurs from Gabon, the Congo Republic, Zaire, Kenya and Tanzania southwards to South West Africa, Botswana, Rhodesia and the Transvaal. It is a tree of woodlands at medium altitudes.

It is a small, semi-deciduous tree, reaching 3 m to 5 m in height, with a very dense, compact, leafy crown. The bark is deeply longitudinally furrowed, thick and corky, and a light creamy brown in colour.

The flowers form dense, terminal heads; they are greenish and inconspicuous and appear from September to November. The fruits, the characteristic monkey-orange, have a thick, hard, woody shell enclosing the fleshy pulp, and mature from July to November.

The branches are armed with rigid, slightly hooked and vicious thorns; it is easy to understand why Africans carry some of these thorns on their persons, believing that they will ward off evil spirits! The bark contains strychnine, and the wood, pliable and tough, is used to make tool handles.

Thirteen other species of *Strychnos* occur in Rhodesia. They are all trees, large shrubs or lianes. *S. cocculoides* is distinguished by its thick, corky bark from the other four Rhodesian species of *Strychnos* with large fruits: *S. spinosa, S. innocua, S. pungens* and *S. madagascariensis*.

VERBENACEAE (LANTANA FAMILY)

54 **VITEX PAYOS** (Lour.) Merr. *Plate 54*

chocolate berry
SH *mutsubvu*
N *umtshwankela*

This species occurs as far north as Kenya and reaches its southern limit in Botswana, Rhodesia and Moçambique.

A tree of woodland and wooded grassland, frequent on rocky slopes, it is perhaps most common at medium altitudes but is also to be found in the Zambezi valley. It is a medium sized, deciduous tree, reaching a maximum height of 10 m, but is usually considerably smaller.

The bark is conspicuously vertically furrowed and is brownish grey in colour. The flowers are attractive, in short, dense heads, and appear in November and December. The fruits, with a hard, blackish brown skin, mature from January to June. Children are fond of the fruits, but this must be one of those childhood pleasures which are soon outgrown as the fruits are not particularly palatable!

Africans use the wood of this tree to provide fire by friction. The leaves are used in African medicine. They are collected, dried and then burned or scalded, and the smoke or steam which rises is inhaled to relieve coughs and asthma.

There are eight or nine other indigenous species of *Vitex* in Rhodesia, of which the most widespread is *V. mombassae*. They are all characterised by the opposite, digitate leaves.

Index of vernacular names

General index